BEHIND THE PEACOCK THRONE

By the same author

THE CACTUS OF LOVE
Travels in Mexico

BLACK MAN'S COUNTRY
Travels in Ghana

THE RED MANDARINS
Travels in China

THE FORGOTTEN VALLEY
Travels in Nepal

DRUMS IN BAHIA
Travels in Brazil

WHILE GOD SLEPT
Travels in Africa

BLACK CAVIAR AND RED OPTIMISM
Travels in Russia

REVOLT IN THE TROPICS
Travels in the Caribbean

SUN, SLAVES AND SINNERS
Travels in the Philippines

BEHIND THE PEACOCK THRONE

by

KARL ESKELUND

ALVIN REDMAN
LONDON

Published by
ALVIN REDMAN LIMITED
17, Fleet Street,
London E.C.4
1965

PRINTED IN GREAT BRITAIN BY
BRISTOL TYPESETTING CO. LTD.
BARTON MANOR - ST. PHILIPS
BRISTOL 2

CONTENTS

Chapter		Page
1	A Toman is a Toman	11
2	The Worshippers of Shaitan	20
3	Words That Beguile Thee	32
4	The Black Eggs	43
5	Tell It to the Shah	52
6	The Sacred City	62
7	Baha'i	75
8	Only on Fridays	86
9	The Old Children	91
10	Persepolis	101
11	The Eternal Flame	109
12	The Thirsty Land	118
13	The Road to Bandarabbas	126
14	The Black Masks	136
15	The Peacock Throne	142
	Index	153

ILLUSTRATIONS

1. Even during the hottest months of the year, it is chilly inside the bazaars, a network of underground streets, each with its own speciality.
2. The wedding is held in a clearing at the foot of the mountain to which Kerend clings.
3. A little girl in the Kurdish camp just outside Kerend. The shoes—which are full of holes—are her father's.
4. Outside all post-offices in Persia sit letter writers to whom people can dictate letters. These " experts " however, do not always understand how to express themselves colourfully.
5. The costly black roe being removed from a small sturgeon in one of the caviar factories along the south coast of the Caspian Sea.
6. The entrance to the Golden Shrine, seen in the background. The blurred quality of the picture is due to the fact that at the same moment I took it, the camera was knocked out of my hands.
7. The mosaic work in Isfahan's mosques is regarded as the finest in the world. The majority of the many beautiful buildings in the city were built by Shah Abbas, about the time of Christian IV.
8. In a tea-house in Isfahan, a passing minstrel tells of his country's history. He knows hundreds of verses by heart —and only now and again casts a sidelong glance towards the open book.
9. The carpet factory in Isfahan. One of the men " in charge " drinks a glass of tea during a break. He looks a good deal older than his thirty-eight years.
10. This was once the entrance to the royal palace of Persepolis. The two animal sculptures with human faces show an Assyrian influence.

11. A village in southern Persia. The rounded roofs are built of clay—thus making roof beams unnecessary, wood being expensive in this part of the country.
12. Unemployment is ever-present in Persia, especially in the south where this picture was taken. Many are peasants out of work because of the drought which has now lasted five years.
13. When the peasants have formed a co-operative society, each family can borrow three hundred tomans from the government. The majority are unable to write their names, so they simply sign the receipt with a fingerprint.
14. A camel caravan passes through an oasis in Persia's vast southern desert.
15. There is something uncanny about the black masks which have a small pin sewn along their middle to keep the shape. The practice probably originates from Arabia.
16. More than two-thirds of Persia is desert and so the camel is still the most important form of transport.

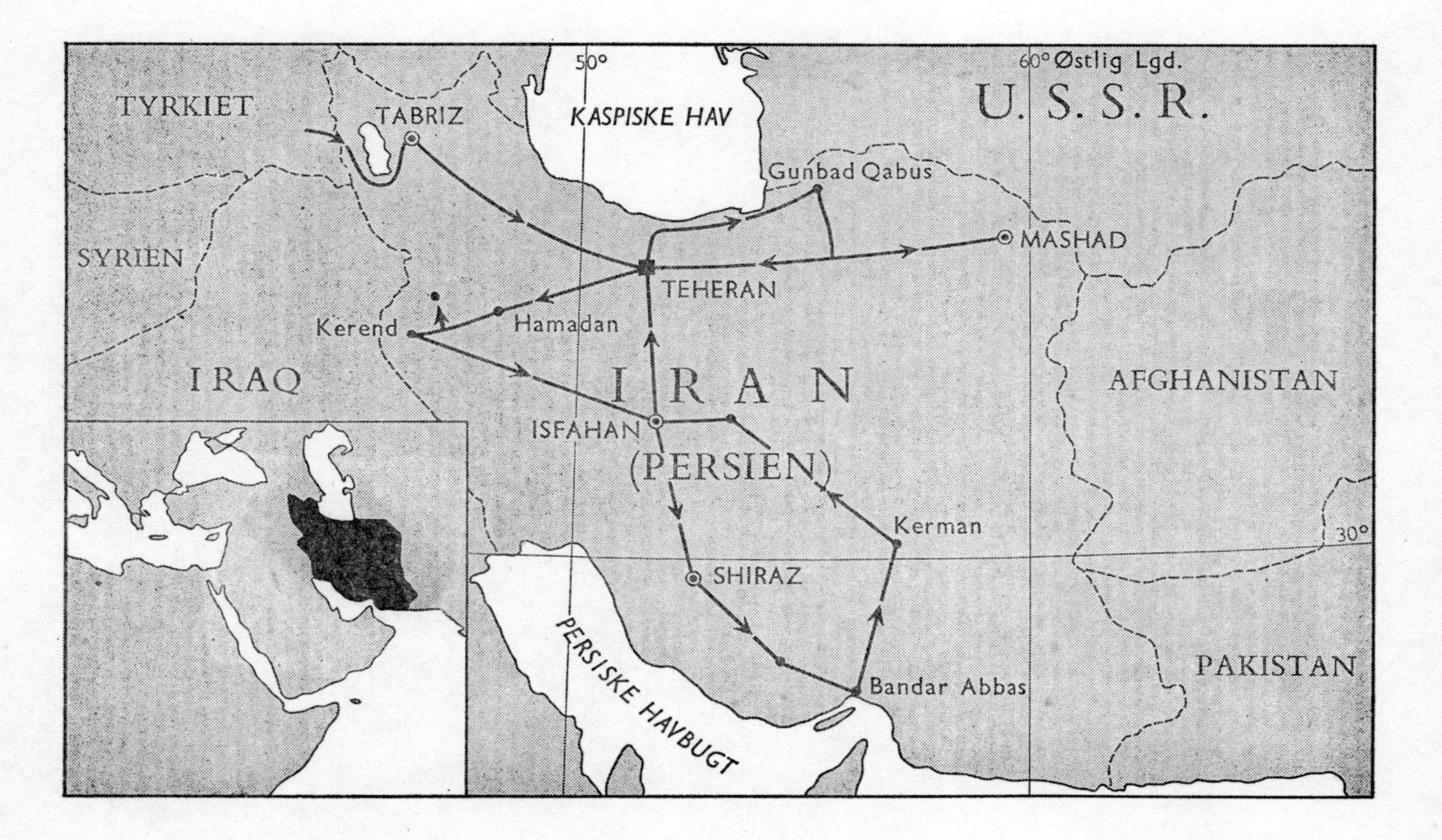
50°
60° Østlig Lgd.
TYRKIET
TABRIZ
KASPISKE HAV
U. S. S. R.
Gunbad Qabus
MASHAD
SYRIEN
TEHERAN
Kerend
Hamadan
IRAQ
I R A N
AFGHANISTAN
ISFAHAN
(PERSIEN)
Kerman
30°
SHIRAZ
PERSISKE HAVBUGT
Bandar Abbas
PAKISTAN

CHAPTER ONE

A TOMAN IS A TOMAN

DAWN WAS JUST beginning to break when we left Erzerun, the last Turkish town before the Persian border. For hours the bus drew a trail of dust across the bare plains and over the mountains. Kurds stared at us from the flat roofs of their clay huts, the women's silver ornaments sparkling in the sun. The men wore loose shirts tied at the waist with coloured sashes.

At noon we reached a wide, deserted valley. On our left, way up north where the Soviet border begins, a snow-covered peak was outlined against the blue sky. It was Ararat, the sacred mountain where Noah landed his ark after the deluge.

Finally some barracks appeared in the barren waste far ahead. "Now we'll soon be there," declared Rashid, a Persian rug dealer who knew a smattering of English. He had crossed the border many times before and so, as a matter of course, had assumed leadership of our motley little group. Apart from Rashid, my Chinese wife and myself, it consisted of a young English couple and four Persian students holiday-bound from their studies in Germany.

The English couple, who were on their way to Australia,

had originally planned to hitch-hike, but had been forced to give it up. Motorists in this part of the world could see no reason why people from the prosperous West should travel free of charge.

At last the bus drew to a stop in front of a long building shared by the Turkish and Persian border authorities. You entered one end with your luggage and—with a bit of luck—emerged at the other some hours later. According to Rashid, this was one of the toughest borders to cross in the whole Middle East, which is saying quite a bit.

As he had predicted, the Turkish half was child's play. It took some time, though, for the officials spoke no word of any foreign language, but they did not try any funny business on us. The Turks, who until a few centuries ago were nomads in Central Asia, are "too primitive to be smart," as Rashid remarked with a note of condescension in his voice.

Getting through ahead of the others, I sat down in a hall in the middle of the building, a kind of no-man's-land with a Turkish sentry at one door, a Persian at the other. Before long an attractive young couple entered, a Dutch woman with her Persian husband. They had visited his parents in Teheran and were now on their way back to London where he studied medicine. When he suggested that we could save the money-exchanger's fee if I gave him my Turkish lira for his Persian tomans (one toman is slightly less than a shilling), I readily agreed.

I still blush at the thought of what happened next. I had said good-bye to the couple and was, from an old habit, recounting the money, when a middle-aged man in smart European clothes entered from the Persian side. He greeted me in a friendly way and, catching sight of the notes, drew nearer. "What does Turkish money look like?" he asked, taking the bunch of notes to have a closer look. I found his behaviour a bit odd, but the next moment he handed the money back to me. They were Persian, so he knew what they looked like, he remarked, waving good-bye to me and disappearing into Turkey.

I thought no more of this incident until Rashid entered a moment later. When he learned at what rate I had exchanged my money he exclaimed that I had been cheated Why on earth had I trusted the word of perfect strangers?

"But they were so nice," I said. "And she was Dutch . . ." I stopped, embarrassed at having revealed my Western immodesty, but Rashid did not seem to mind in the least.

"She may be Dutch, but her husband is a Persian," he said. "You must never trust anyone from this part of the world." This made me take out my newly-acquired tomans and finish counting them—slowly at first, then faster, and finally feverishly.

"Anything wrong?" Rashid asked anxiously. I was about to say yes, everything was wrong, but checked myself. Had I owned up to letting another perfect stranger pinch two hundred-toman notes right under my nose, he would probably have considered me insane. No, everything was all right, I lied, and not until many days later did I gather enough courage to confess to my wife what a sucker I had been.

We waited until the others had joined us and then advanced in battle array. This was the plan of Rashid, who had noticed on his previous trips that the Persian officials did not like to ask for bribes from Europeans. We had therefore agreed that he and the students were to stay glued to either the English couple or to me. Being an Oriental, my wife could hardly be expected to have a restraining influence on the officials.

It worked beautifully with the Customs officials, but the passport inspector, who had probably been informed of our conspiracy, proved more astute. Collecting our passports, he pushed them aside and began practising his atrocious English on us as he noisily imbibed glass after glass of hot tea. Every once in a while a tall fellow in a crumpled suit would enter and whisper into his ear.

Rashid soon figured out what was going on. The tall man, who was postmaster in a Persian town some fifteen miles away, had a postal bus waiting outside. If we were delayed until the departure of the regular afternoon bus we would be at his mercy, for there was no other connection until next morning.

It was so well-timed that when we finally emerged from the building, we could see the regular afternoon bus disappearing in a cloud of dust. After letting us stand for a few minutes in the icy mountain wind, the postmaster sauntered over and offered to take us to town.

A lengthy discussion now followed between Rashid and the postmaster, who demanded five tomans a head for the ride, or twice the normal fare. Each held a string of prayer beads in his hand, and the angrier they became the faster their fingers counted the beads. Finally Rashid picked up his suitcase and strode indignantly back to the building from which we had just escaped. We would spend the night in a dormitory maintained by the border authorities, he had decided. The others followed him readily, but I protested that my wife and I were exhausted and wanted to spend the night at a proper hotel . . .

" Sh-sh-sh! " admonished Chi-yun, who is usually very polite, but the Oriental in her rebelled against the way I spoiled Rashid's game. " Just pretend you don't mind sleeping here," she added under her breath, and I obediently picked up our suitcases. This may have contributed to the final capitulation of the postmaster, who suddenly broke down and offered to take us to town for two and a half tomans each. That was the regular price, but Rashid, having once gained the upper hand, saw no reason for relinquishing it so easily. " Two tomans," he said firmly, and the postmaster had to swallow the bitter pill with a smile.

The sun had already set when we finally reached the little border town. In the darkness we caught a glimpse of open sewers along a dusty main street which led to a tiny unkempt park with a statue of the Shah in the centre. Rashid protested vehemently at my suggestion that the driver take us directly to the best hotel. Then we would surely be overcharged, he asserted, but if we went around and inquired first we could get lodgings very cheaply.

I was permitted to accompany him on the condition that I kept out of sight while negotiations were going on. Everybody knew that Europeans had no patience, and the mere sight of me would raise the price.

At the town's four hotels, which were also tea-houses, radios blared the same sad, vibrating strains one hears throughout the Arab world. The customers, all males, sat cross-legged on thick rugs and chatted as a water-pipe passed from mouth to mouth. Many had clean-shaven heads and wore skull-caps. In a long row outside the door stood their worn canvas shoes with up-turned toes.

The few women we saw in the street were carrying water from a public pump. Only the arm supporting the jug was visible, the rest being hidden beneath the *chadur,* as the Persians call the cloak-like garment which the women wrap around themselves.

Rashid claimed that the hotel where we finally decided to stay was the best in the town. That may be so, but I'll never forget the face of the young Englishman when, on asking where one could bathe, he was shown a battered wash-basin in the corridor which served all the guests. You only had to follow your nose to get to the lavatory, an enclosure with a hole in the floor. In lieu of toilet paper, which is not used in Mohammedan countries, there was a water jug with a long spout.

The friendly proprietor was puzzled by our indignation at finding soiled sheets on our bed. You can secure clean bedding at provincial hotels in Persia by paying a couple of tomans extra, but this we did not know yet. In the hope of soothing my temper he fetched an almost clean towel, and covered our greasy pillow with it.

While we were changing our clothes my wife suddenly jumped to one side and shouted for me to turn off the light. There were no curtains, and the guests at the tea-house across the street seemed disappointed to be cheated of the climax of a free strip-tease show.

Rashid succeeded in beating the price of our dinner down to half of what the proprietor first demanded. We had delicious mutton grilled on the spit and served with raw onion, raw egg-yolk, rice and flat, unleavened bread.

1. Even during the hottest months of the year, it is chilly inside the bazaars, a network of underground streets, each with its own speciality.

2. The wedding is held in a clearing at the foot of the mountain to which Kerend clings.

3. A little girl in the Kurdish camp just outside Kerend. The shoes – which are full of holes – are her father's.

4. Outside all post-offices in Persia sit letter writers to whom people can dictate letters. These "experts", however, do not always understand how to express themselves colourfully.

As we were drinking our tea after dinner, a plain-clothes man came in and asked to see our papers. He explained that it was not sufficient for foreigners to possess a visa. At Tabriz, the first large town which we came to, we would have to stop and ask the police for permission to proceed to Teheran. If later on we wanted to travel outside the capital we would also have to obtain permission.

"He was from the Shah's secret police," one of the students whispered when the man had gone. "They are everywhere."

"Yes, it's wise not to talk politics," Rashid broke in and then began telling us about his plans for the following day. The mail bus by which we had come from the border was going on to Teheran, and he had already arranged for us to go along at a cheaper rate.

Next morning the postmaster showed up in person to collect our fares. At the last moment he suddenly demanded that we pay extra for the front seats. But as soon as Rashid reached for his suitcase, he threw in the towel.

All that day the bus tore over a plateau which seemed to become more dry and sandy by the hour. Every now and then a seemingly endless row of mounds would appear, stretching across the flat, monotonous landscape. That was earth taken from the underground canals, or *quanats*, through which water came flowing from distant mountains. Everywhere in Persia, with the exception of the humid Caspian Sea area, the farmers depend on the *quanats*, which in some places reach a length of close on a hundred miles.

Several times we passed blind beggars who sat in the middle of nowhere. Hearing a car approach, they would raise their arms in supplication. Those who gave them a mite would receive a blessing in return, but our bus was in a hurry and not once did we stop.

We spent the night at Tabriz, a large provincial town with one-storeyed houses along wide, tree-lined streets. Before leaving in the morning we went to the bazaar with Rashid who wanted to check up on prices of rugs. For a long time we wandered about in the covered streets which were already beginning to get crowded, though the sun had just risen. Between the stalls were tiny workshops where everything from furniture and shoes to primitive kitchen utensils was produced by hand. I have often bemoaned the success of plastic, but the sight of a man hammering away to turn the cover of an oil drum into a washbasin makes you change your point of view.

Curiosity made me go down some steep, narrow stairs in a remote corner of the bazaar. They led to a dark cellar where two boys were busy making cotton thread. One turned a large, creaking wheel while the other ran back and forth, to fasten the threads to wooden posts. Their faces had a sickly pallor, and no wonder. They worked down there from sunrise to sundown, we learned through Rashid. The older one, who was ten, earned one toman a day, his seven-year-old colleague slightly over half a toman.

For the rest of the day I kept seeing the two little boys. Rashid told us that he had been just as poor during his childhood. We began to understand why the struggle for a toman could be so grim.

Late in the afternoon we finally reached Teheran. The city looked lovely as it lay at the foot of a majestic, snow-covered mountain range, golden in the last rays of the sun. From a shabby district of low clay huts we reached a broad boulevard running between tall modern buildings. The first neon lights began to glow against the darkening sky.

We now had to part with our travelling companions who were going to a cheap hotel recommended by Rashid. Chi-yun and I thought we deserved a little luxury and went to a big, expensive hotel. I didn't bat an eye when the receptionist told me that a room with a bath cost 110 tomans a day, or more than five pounds, but suddenly I saw Rashid's face before me.

" I'll pay sixty tomans," I said. " That is out of the question," the receptionist replied stiffly, but seeing me reach for my suitcase he quickly added that we could discuss the matter. " What about ninety?"

" Seventy," I declared brusquely, and he agreed with a nod. Involuntarily I straightened myself. Rashid would have been proud of me.

CHAPTER TWO

THE WORSHIPPERS OF SHAITAN

EVERY MORNING AT dawn an express bus leaves Teheran for the south-western part of the country. After crossing a stony desert, it reaches a chain of barren mountains. The engines often start boiling on the steep curves, but the drivers just raise the bonnets and drive on with their heads sticking out of the windows.

In a green mountain valley high above sea level lies Hamadan, or Ekbatana as the town was called in ancient times when it rivalled Babylon. It was here Cyrus the Great, founder of the Persian empire, won his first decisive victory. It was also near here that Alexander the Great, a couple of centuries later, crushed the Persian armies, thus opening the way to India.

A weather-worn inscription in the mountains high above the road proclaims that Darius, greatest of the Persian rulers, came by on one of his military campaigns. He was then at the height of his power and would undoubtedly have scoffed if told that a Macedonian warrior was soon to put an end to his dynasty.

After the mountains you again reach a hot plain. Gigantic dust columns whirl about like dervishes. As you are watching them they suddenly disintegrate and are gone like the genie of the bottle . . .

Late in the afternoon we went off together with our interpreter, a jolly young Persian by the name of Abdul. About a mile off the main road a furrowed rock rose above the plain. On the slope, brown clay huts lay like steps, one man's roof forming the next man's front yard. That was Kerend, our destination, but the road leading there was so poor that the driver did not dare to go all the way.

Fortunately we had no more luggage than we could easily carry ourselves. We became more and more entranced as we approached the town. With its narrow lanes zigzagging up the rocky slope, it looked as if it had come straight out of the Middle Ages.

It was not quite so untouched, for above the houses hung a maze of electric wires. A letter of introduction which we brought from a Persian friend in Teheran turned out to be for the manager of the electricity plant. His home lay at the foot of the rock; it was of clay like the other huts, but had real glass windows instead of shutters and was surrounded by a high wall.

We were immediately invited inside by the young manager whose bushy moustache contrasted strangely with a striped European suit. It surprised us that his wife and mother did not pull the *chadur* in front of their faces as most Persian women do when receiving strangers of the opposite sex. The two younger ones of the family's three children began howling at the sight of us.

There were no chairs, but luxurious rugs covered the floor. After having served tea the women withdrew to the kitchen, a dark shed across the dusty courtyard.

We asked the manager to help us find a suitable hotel, but he insisted that we be his guests. I must admit that we did not put up much of a resistance, for we wanted more than anything else to live in a Persian home.

The room where we sat was put at our disposal. Usually our host and hostess slept here, but they would move into the next room with the old lady and the children. The weather was still mild, so Abdul could sleep on the veranda.

There were no beds in sight. They were hardly ever used outside the large towns, Abdul explained. People slept on the floor like they do in Japan.

Though born in Kerend, our host could not tell us how many people there were in the town (close to ten thousand, we later learned). He only knew that some six hundred homes were electrified, the rest still used oil lamps. Most of the inhabitants were farmers whose fields were watered by a stream which came out of the rocks and rushed down through the city to disappear a few miles away, absorbed by the thirsty earth.

The women began quietly to set the table—that is to say they spread a cloth on the rug, for most Persians also eat on the floor. Chi-yun and I waited anxiously for the food. Until now we had eaten at restaurants, and just about the only thing you could get was mutton roasted on a spit, the Persian equivalent of our steak. We were crazy about it at first, but now we had been in the country for two weeks.

We drew a sigh of relief when the women brought in a delicious stew of mutton and vegetables followed by fried chicken, goat cheese and a melon as sweet as honey.

Our hostess and her mother-in-law shyly declined to eat

with us. Only modern city people sat with the menfolk when there were guests, Abdul told us.

After dinner we were again served tea—some Persians drink as many as fifty glasses a day. Through the open door we could see the moon hanging like a silver disc above the rock. It was only eight o'clock, but the city lay in darkness. From the time before electricity was installed, the inhabitants had kept their habit of retiring with the sun.

By the time we went to bed, the children had begun to overcome their shyness. The one in the middle, a lovely girl with silver earrings, settled down on Chi-yun's lap and fell asleep there.

The women quickly made our beds on the floor. Just as I was about to fall asleep I heard Chi-yun's voice. "What an awful racket the dogs are making outside," she said.

"Put some cotton-wool in your ears," I muttered.

"It sounds as if there are lots of them," she went on. "That's funny—after all, one rarely sees a dog here in Persia."

Yes, that was funny, I thought sleepily. The Prophet said that dogs were unclean, so Mohammedans avoid keeping them . . .

We woke up when the first grey light came creeping in through the windows. A rooster belatedly crowed the new day in, and slowly the light turned golden.

"Don't you miss something?" Chi-yun suddenly asked me.

"No, what should that be?"

"We haven't heard the usual call for prayers."

"That's right," I exclaimed. In all the Persian towns

we had visited we had heard the chanting call for prayers every morning at dawn.

"We must find out why they don't do it here," I continued, sitting up. While we washed ourselves at the pump in the yard, the members of the family came out one by one, filled a jar with water and proceeded to the old-fashioned lavatory. The women had already lit a fire in the kitchen and soon served a delicious breakfast of oatmeal boiled in sour milk and sheep's fat.

Weren't there exceptionally many dogs in Kerend? I asked our host during the meal. He nodded, but offered no explanation. "And we haven't heard any call for prayers," I continued. "Perhaps we were still sleeping and missed it?"

No, they had no call for prayers in Kerend. Why was that? After a moment of hesitation he replied that the people of this town had their own customs. He was not very interested in religion and so could not tell us much about it, but we could ask the caretaker of the mosque.

After breakfast, when we went for a walk in the town, heads popped out from doorways and windows to stare at us. Even when we looked directly at the women they did not cover their faces. Abdul usually claims to be very modern, but we could tell that this shocked him a bit.

We noticed another peculiar thing—there did not seem to be a single man in town who did not have a moustache.

Water came flowing through the open sewer that ran along the main street. It turned pink, then dark red—the butcher had just stuck his knife into the throat of a bleating lamb, and he skinned and quartered it right in the middle of the street. The steady hammering of anvils stopped for a moment as we passed the blacksmiths; like the Orient, each trade was gathered together in its own section. The baker was taking his round, flat loaves out of the oven, which had been hollowed into the rocks. A Jewish rug dealer with a long white beard beckoned us.

"It doesn't cost anything to have a look," he shouted.

Above the town we found the mosque, an insignificant-looking clay building without a cupola. We couldn't learn much from the old caretaker who accompanied us into the room, which was empty except for some threadbare carpets. They did not call for prayers because no mullah was attached to the mosque, he said (a mullah is a Mohammedan teacher of religion). There was no pulpit, and he could not even remember when the last service had been held, yet he maintained that the inhabitants were no different from other Mohammedans. "Just less religious," he said.

"No mullah, no sermon—that's very strange," Abdul muttered as we left. "And did you notice the bottles?"

On a shelf inside the building he had seen some bottles of arak, as firewater is called in the Middle East. Mohammed prohibited his followers from taking intoxicating drinks, so a mosque was the last place one would expect to find hard liquor.

"But of course there may only have been water in the bottles," Abdul added.

On a hill close to the town we found the graveyard. It had little in common with the pleasant gardens where the dead find their last resting place in the West. In Persia it is difficult enough to find water for the living, so the dead have to manage without. Gravestones by the hundred sprouted from the bone-dry earth, but not a single blade of grass.

On some of the old tombstones we discovered crude carvings of fighting warriors. This perplexed Abdul, as it is strictly prohibited for Mohammedans to depict the human form.

We had a leisurely afternoon, but the next morning the old town came suddenly to life. Gaily-dressed people thronged the streets, which resounded with gay music of horns and drums. Following the sound, we came to a courtyard where people were dancing in a long line, accompanied by the noisiest three-man orchestra I had ever heard. The drummers banged away with their sticks and the flute player looked as if his cheeks would burst. Brightly-coloured skirts billowed around the ankles of the women, whose silver ornaments jingled as they skipped and hopped.

The surrounding roofs had been covered with rugs, and here sat the spectators, eating and drinking merrily. When the rhythm became especially inciting, one of the dancers would jump out of the line and perform a solo as everybody clapped in time with the music.

It was a wedding feast, and some of the guests immediately made room for us on one of the roofs. Dish after dish of food was passed to us: fried mutton and chicken, cucumbers and melons, grapes, cheese and nuts. Each one of us was given a huge slug of arak and our neighbours raised their glasses. It burned all the way down, but it felt good.

When I rose to go down and photograph the dancers, Chi-yun took my pocketbook and put it in her purse. Abdul saw it and smiled. "You don't have to worry about pickpockets here," he said.

"But you yourself told us just the other day that there are thieves everywhere."

"Yes, but here we are guests. Then it is quite different."

A flock of barefoot children trailed after me as I climbed down. I was trying to push them aside and take a picture, when a policeman placed himself in front of me with his arms and legs spread out. "No picture taking is permitted," he said sternly. My explanation that I was a journalist made no impression whatever on him, but when he heard that I was the guest of the manager of the electric plant he broke into a smile. That was different! I was welcome to take as many pictures as I pleased, and to demonstrate his goodwill he began chasing away the kids clustered around me.

Everybody cheered when Chi-yun and I joined the dancers. She caught the rhythm right away, but I could not for the life of me follow the simple steps. The spectators politely refrained from laughing at me.

In the midst of this the door to one of the huts was opened and the bridegroom came out. He was very young, with only a hint of a moustache, and a shy smile spread across his face as everybody began clapping and shouting. Then his comrades ran over and slapped him on the back, and while a spirited march was played he circulated among the guests, each of whom pressed a banknote in his hand. Finally he had so many that he could hardly hold them. All newly-weds were given such a start in life here in Kerend, a guest told us. Abdul, who had travelled far and wide in Persia, had never heard of the custom before.

As I was walking around with my camera, Abdul came and put a hand on my shoulder. He hated to say it, but a relative of the groom had hinted that we had better go now.

Many of the guests nodded to us as we walked away, but even so we had a feeling that they were relieved at our departure.

"Could it be because they don't want me to see the bride?" I asked Abdul.

"I don't think so—or they would have asked your wife to stay. I think something is going to take place that they don't want us to see."

At dinner we tried to get some more information from our host, but he just smiled and began to talk about something else. The following afternoon we were luckier. In the main street we met two dusty, bearded young fellows carrying knapsacks. They spoke English and told us that they were on a two-weeks' leave from the university of Teheran where they studied ancient religions. Their professor had told them to find out all they could about the local beliefs. It did not surprise them to hear of our failure to get anywhere with the people here.

"They are devil-worshippers," they whispered, using the Arab word *Shaitan*. "The people keep their religion secret because they were once persecuted by the Mohammedans."

Some years ago, a German and an English scholar of ancient religions had visited the town, but without learning much, they continued. Only a couple of short, rather incomplete scientific studies had been written about the religion of Kerend. In the hope of getting better results, the two students had pretended to belong to the sect.

"That's why we have grown whiskers," they explained with boyish enthusiasm. "Haven't you noticed that all the men in Kerend have moustaches?"

We nodded. The two students had tried to find the reason

for this, but without success. Most probably a holy man from here had once worn a moustache.

As far as is known, the roots of the strange religion go back to the times before the Arab conquest of Persia in the seventh century. In those days there were many Christians in Persia, but the majority were fire-worshippers or Zarathustrians. They were converted to Islam, but some continued to practise their old religion in secret.

" It must have been difficult," one of the students said. " They had to pose as Mohammedans and at the same time had to prevent true Mohammedans from settling down here lest they found out. They managed to keep this guise by claiming to be a special Moslem sect. If you ask them whether they are Mohammedans, they always say yes, but it certainly is not true."

He mentioned several points which we had noticed ourselves—the figures on the tombstones, the reluctance of the townsmen to let strangers witness their religious ceremonies, and the fact that the women did not cover their faces.

" And then their fires," the other added. " On special occasions they light fires up in the hills. This undoubtedly comes from the ancient fire-worshippers—they always had a fire burning in their temples, which were usually situated on hilltops."

Ali-Haq, the sect is called, meaning " Adherents of Ali ". In Persia, however, there is a tendency to confound Ali with God, just as some Christians can hardly distinguish between God and Jesus. Ali-Haq can therefore also mean " Children of God ", and the two students felt certain that this had been the original meaning.

Early one morning in a neighbouring village they had

seen people standing outside their houses wearing white undergarments. The fire-worshippers had also prayed to the rising sun, and always clad in white underwear.

At another place the villagers had rushed over to prevent one of the students from killing a scorpion. They had told a bewildering story of some people and animals who, long ago, had been saved from drowning by seeking refuge in a large boat. When the vessel struck a rock, a hole was torn in the bottom and everybody would have drowned but for a brave scorpion, which plugged the hole with its body (it cannot have been a very large hole!). That was why no one should ever kill a scorpion.

Everywhere in the world people tell legends about the great deluge, but this was the oddest one Chi-yun and I had heard as yet.

Why had the students called the members of the Ali-Haq sect devil-worshippers? Because to them, evil was fully as important as good. An old man had told them that man had no reason to fear the power of good, which by its very nature was incapable of doing evil, but with Shaitan it was another matter. He was dangerous, so it was important to keep on the right side of him.

When the sect sacrificed a sheep, it was to propitiate Shaitan. It was forbidden ever to mention his name, because then he would become angry and strike people blind. The students also thought that the infrequent religious services in Kerend were mainly held in honour of the Lord of Evil. They had not succeeded in attending such a service, but had heard that a member of the sect usually fell into a trance. Shaitan would then speak through the medium, it was believed.

This way of thinking may also have originated with the ancient fire-worshippers, who believed that the universe was divided between good and evil forces constantly at war with each other. It was the duty of the fire-worshippers to support the powers of good, but the Ali-Haqs seemed to have come to the conclusion that it was even more important to secure the goodwill of the evil one.

The sect did not participate in the yearly Mohammedan fast of one month. On the contrary, many of them feasted during this period. Nor did they keep the young people so strictly apart as the Mohammedans. They were even permitted to get acquainted before they were married—something unheard of except in ultra-modern circles in big cities. It was also said that the Ali-Haqs had once had a female leader, but the students had not been able to get this confirmed.

That was about all we could learn from the two boys, who were now going back to Teheran. We accompanied them down to the main road, where they soon caught a bus. As we walked back to Kerend we could still hear music from the wedding, which was to last for three days. That evening we saw a fire on top of the hill where the graveyard was situated.

"It must be in connection with the wedding," I said to the manager of the electric plant. Being a polite host, he nodded and smiled, but said no more.

CHAPTER THREE

WORDS THAT BEGUILE THEE

THE DOGS CAUGHT our scent long before we reached the little encampment of the nomads. They came dashing towards us, barking furiously, and then ran around us in a steadily diminishing circle as if they were herding sheep. Abdul tried to put on a brave front, but he was trembling with fear. He comes from Mashhad, a holy city where one occasionally comes across camels in the middle of the town, but never a dog.

Some figures now emerged from the low, dark tents. They called out to the dogs, which quickly ran back and flopped down in the shade, panting, their long tongues hanging out. They had done their duty.

To our disappointment, the men were dressed in European jackets—a prestige symbol throughout the underdeveloped world—but the rest of their costume was quite dramatic. They wore long, baggy trousers tied tightly round the ankles and held round the waist with broad sashes. The long fringes of their headcloths came all the way down to their deep-set eyes.

" *Salam*! " Abdul greeted them.

" *Salam alaikum* "—peace be with you also—they replied,

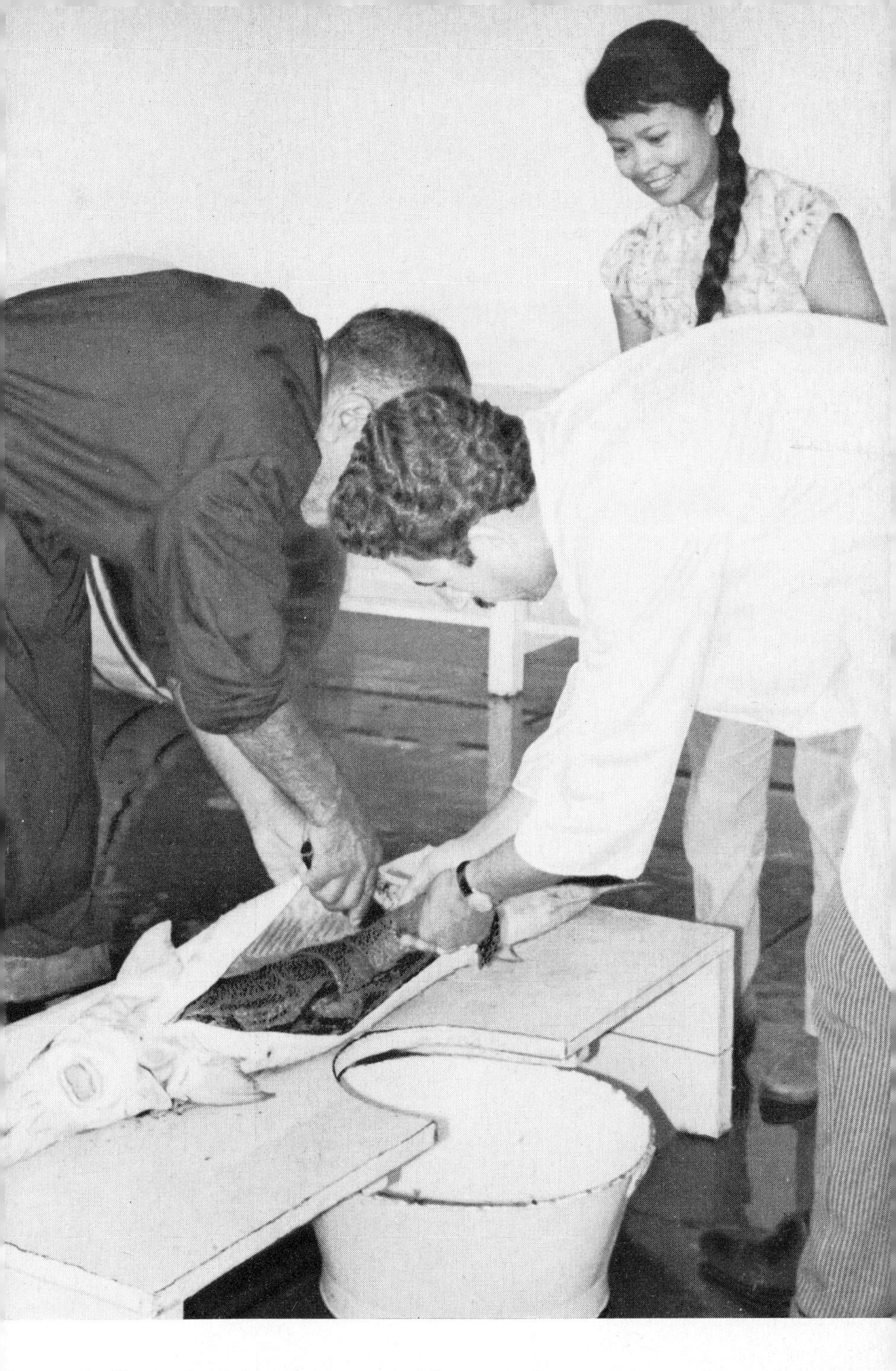

5. The costly black roe being removed from a small sturgeon in one of the caviar factories along the south coast of the Caspian Sea.

6. The entrance to the Golden Spire, seen in the background. The blurred quality of the picture is due to the fact that at the same moment I took it, the camera was knocked out of my hands.

raising the right hand to the forehead and then lowering it to the chest with a slight bow. When we had introduced ourselves, the leader of the camp, a grey-haired man by the name of Baisger, invited us to his tent.

Inside a circular enclosure of straw mats in front of his tent sat some women. Some of them were weaving, others were pushing big needles through thick cloth soles for Persian slippers. One was rocking a bag made of sheepskin, with the fur still on. It was suspended from a crudely constructed tripod of branches, and whey was trickling down on the ground as it sloshed back and forth, for she was churning butter. Two thick plaits of her hair dangled like pendulums over her dirty velvet dress.

The children clung to their mothers, frightened at the sight of the strangers. Each one wore an amulet around the neck, a small leather pouch containing perhaps a stone from the grave of a saint or a scrap of paper with a sacred text from the Koran.

The walls of the woollen tent did not reach all the way down to the ground, so every breath of wind could enter and cool you off. From a pile of rugs Baisger picked the finest one and spread it out on the ground for us. The moment we sat down the flies came, settling in lumps at the corners of the eyes and mouth. We struck savagely at them, but they did not seem to bother the nomads.

When the women had brought us tea they returned to the enclosure. The men, who had sat down in a semi-circle around us, were all lean and sinewy, with long, narrow faces dominated by hawk-like noses. They smelled of sheep.

Persian etiquette calls for polite talk about wind and weather until the first glass of tea has been emptied, so after swallowing a few sips of the scalding liquid I opened the conversation by expressing surprise that they all had grey eyes. Somehow one expects to find dark people in this part of the world.

Abdul, who had gone to middle school and loved to show off his knowledge, immediately commenced a lecture on the background of our hosts. They were Kurds, the largest tribe in the Middle East. Thousands of years ago, this Aryan people came wandering from the north with their flocks. Some went to India, where they became lords of the dark Dravidians by setting themselves up as Brahmins—the priestly caste. Others settled down in the Middle East and became the Kurds of today. Between four and five million of them are living in the mountainous border lands between Turkey, Iraq, Persia, Syria and the Soviet Union. They profess to be Mohammedans, but are so only on the surface . . .

Here I broke in to ask Baisger what *he* knew about the origin of his people. He began to cough violently, having lit by mistake the filter end of the cigarette we had offered him. Regaining his breath he began to tell us about a great king, Solomon, who had lived many, many years ago . . .

Solomon? Was that the same king who had once ruled over the Jews?

This he did not know, but anyhow, one day this great king had felt a desire for light-skinned women, so he had sent a band of warriors off to the north to procure some. They flew through the air . . .

"*Flew* through the air?" I repeated, glancing severely at Abdul. Had our host used this expression, or was it something he himself had invented? It was necessary for me to ask, for we had discovered that Abdul was possessed by a desire to embellish facts. It did not matter so much that he automatically multiplied all sums, but when he indulged in flights of fancy we simply had to pull him down to earth again. Even when we caught him in the act he was not in the least bit embarrassed. At first I had given him hell, but then my wife had explained that he really did it for my sake, having discovered that my face brightened every time I found something colourful to write about. His exaggerations no longer angered me, but I just had to make a sample test every once in a while.

"Yes, that's exactly what he said, *flew* through the air!" Abdul answered triumphantly. Judging by the expression of the others, this was considered a normal mode of travelling in those distant days, at least for attendants of great lords. When the warriors returned they learned that their king had departed, so they married the light-haired beauties themselves, and thus their descendants, the Kurds, were light and had grey eyes . . .

A child began to cry. An old woman pulled out her withered breast and stuck it into the mouth of the little one, who sucked greedily, taking it for the real thing, and then fell asleep.

When I began talking about the fame of the Kurds as warriors, our hosts straightened themselves proudly. That they still exist as a people is little short of a miracle, for they seem to be possessed of a suicidal desire to challenge fate. The first time they made their appearance in history was several hundred years before the birth of Christ, when ten thousand Greek soldiers were on their way home after participating in a Persian civil war. The Athenian historian,

Xenophon, who took part in the campaign, tells that the Greeks were constantly harassed by wild " Karduchis ", as the Kurds were called in those days.

Later they hurled themselves with savage fury against anyone who encroached on their domain. As far as is known, Alexander the Great had to protect his flank against them on his march through Persia. Even Genghis Khan, who crushed everything that lay in his path, could not control them, and Timur the Terrible of Samarkand learned to avoid their grazing grounds on his marches to Babylon or Asia Minor.

When the Ottoman Empire was dissolved after the first World War, the Kurds sent a delegate to Versailles requesting permission to form an independent state. Nobody would listen to them, so they remained under the Turks, Iraqis, Persians, Syrians and Russians.

That did not deter them, however. They denounced their masters as oppressors, and years passed before the resistance of the stubborn nomads was finally broken.

The struggle was fiercest in Turkey. About one and a half million Kurds were living in the eastern part of the country, but the government simply denied their existence and called them " mountain Turks ". When the Kurds as stubbornly showed that they truly did exist, the Turks attempted to wipe them out. They had had good practice in this from their massacres of Armenian and Greek minorities. Quietly they murdered about half a million Kurds. Since then, the survivors have been lying low.

In Iraq the government has never really succeeded in subduing the large groups of Kurds who inhabit the mountainous region in the north of the country. Time and again

Baghdad has announced that now the Kurdish problem has been solved—but when spring comes, the Kurds rise again. Perhaps they are like the old Vikings—when the winter is over they begin to itch for action.

In Persia the Kurds have not been such a great problem, mainly because the government used to close its eyes indulgently when they did a bit of highway robbery on the side. The nomads have always considered it their natural right to help the despised city dwellers get rid of their earthly possessions. When the Kurds went too far, Teheran would send a punitive expedition against them, but the government was usually too weak to enforce its will in the desert.

All this was changed in the early twenties by the father of the present Shah, an officer by the name of Reza. Not without justice is he known as the creator of modern Persia, or Iran, as he insisted on calling it. In a few years he united the country which is about the size of England, France, Spain and Germany put together. He brought order to the hopelessly jumbled finances and built roads and railways. Teheran was changed from a sleepy, overgrown village into a modern metropolis. He broke the hold of the mullahs on the ignorant people, tore the veil off the women, and showed the nomads who was master of the country. Thousands were executed, tens of thousands exiled to remote parts of the country.

The Kurds also felt the iron hand of Reza Shah. Even so, Baisger's eyes shone with admiration as he told us how the great Shah once had some notorious Kurdish bandits immured alive in the rocks of a mountain pass where they had committed many of their crimes. Baisger had once gone there with his father. All you could see of the robbers was their shrunken heads.

"Always obey your Shah," his father had admonished him, "else you may suffer the same fate as these people."

Baisger had never forgotten these words, but he was no longer so sure that it was wise to be obedient. Yes, under the old Shah—as long as he ruled, there had been justice. He never broke his word. But many things had changed since his son, Mohammed Reza, had mounted the throne twenty years ago . . .

The others nodded darkly. Yes, there was no justice any more. They did not have a word to say against the young Shah (at forty-five, Mohammed Reza is still called "the young one"). He probably did not know what was going on, but his aides must be bad people.

Why? The nomads told us that some years ago the young Shah had ordered all the tribespeople to turn in their arms. Those who did not obey were threatened with dire punishment.

"We obeyed," Baisger said slowly. "But another tribe who had been our enemies for years refused to lay down their arms. And what happened to them? Were they punished as the great Shah would have done?"

Baisger looked at the others, who shook their heads so energetically that the tassels danced on their foreheads.

"No, and they are far better off than we who obeyed," he continued. "They have withdrawn into the mountains over there." He pointed towards the north where a chain of dark mountains rose above the plain. "There they sit in comfort, supported by the young Shah!"

This sounded incredible, but I later learned through

other sources that the government does indeed send money occasionally to some bands of wild Kurds who live up in the mountains north of Kerend. This is a kind of "Danegeld" to restrain them from plundering on the main roads.

But the worst of it was that their enemies had taken over vast grazing grounds that used to belong to them, Baisger continued. "We could easily have settled the score with them in the old days," he added, clenching his fist. "But now we have no arms. We have to manage with the grazing grounds which they have no use for."

That was why their little group did not have nearly as many sheep as before. From a couple of thousand, their flock had dwindled to four hundred. That was not nearly enough for the fifty-two people of their camp, so they had rented a plot of land from a wealthy man in Kerend. As was customary in this area, they had received a third of the harvest. Slowly agriculture had become their most important source of income.

Then came the young Shah's land reform. It had begun when they were up in the pastures in the relatively cool highlands west of here. As soon as they heard that the Shah would visit the provincial capital to distribute the land, Baisger and two other men had gone there.

They had never been in a large city before and had gaped at the tall buildings and the many motor-cars. Everybody applauded when the Shah stepped out on a grandstand decorated with flowers. He made a speech promising land to those who did not have any and then he handed out deeds stating that the recipients now owned the land they worked on.

Baisger and his two companions had stood there a long

time, waiting for their names to be called. Finally there were no more deeds, and still they had not received any land. As the Shah was about to leave they rushed towards him, elbowing their way through the crowd.

When they had almost reached the Shah they were stopped by some soldiers in splendid uniforms. They were Kurds—all the Shah's bodyguards are—but even so they had pushed them rudely aside.

"We have to talk to the Shah," Baisger had shouted. "He has forgotten us!"

"Write to the Minister of Agriculture," shouted an official who had heard them. Baisger and his friends then went to one of the professional letter-writers who sat in front of the post office and dictated a letter explaining how they had been overlooked.

Two months later the reply came. There had been no mistake, it said, since only farmers who lived on one spot were entitled to receive land.

Their savings had gone to pay for the trip to the provincial capital, but nothing could be done about that. When autumn came and the tribe went down as usual to work the piece of land which they leased from the wealthy man in Kerend, they found that great changes had taken place. Before the land distribution, the landlord in Kerend had not actually owned the land, but rented it from a big landowner and then sublet it to the nomads. He did not dare to do this any more, for during the land reform the land had been given to him, and a new law forbade him to farm it out. As a result, he would only employ the nomads as farm-hands, paying them three tomans a day. That would have been all right if there had been plenty of work, but usually he could use only one or two of them. The rest went without work for weeks on end.

Many others were unemployed now, for shortly before the land reform the landowners had discovered an escape clause which permitted them to keep all the land which they cultivated with machinery and hired labour. Many had consequently purchased tractors and harvesters, so there was much less need for labour than before.

" We can't get more grazing grounds, and we can't find work," Baisger said. " It is worse for the young men. How can they ever save enough money to get a wife?"

A wife cost beween one and two hundred tomans. Formerly, each man received a small sum of money when they shared the profits after the harvest, but now it was impossible to put anything aside. All the money they earned went for rice and wheat. There were four marriageable young men in the camp who did not have any prospect of obtaining a bride.

One misfortune led to another. A married man was exempted from military service—but not a bachelor. You could buy yourself out of it for a couple of hundred tomans, but none of the young men had so much money—or they would have bought a wife . . .

Here Baisger looked at me and added hopefully that now things might improve for them. Through the foreign guest, the Shah would learn how unjustly they had been treated. They would be given land . . .

" Say, they seem to be under the impression that we can help them," I said to Abdul.

" Yes," he replied cheerfully, " they think we are connected with the government."

"You must explain to them that they are mistaken."

"That would be a pity."

"But we can't help them!"

"What does that matter, as long as they think so?" he replied with a smile, and a little later, when we were on our way back to Kerend, he recited a poem for us written many hundred years ago by Saadi, one of the greatest of the Persian poets:

Words which beguile thee
But thy heart make glad
Outvalue truth
Which makes thy temper sad.

CHAPTER FOUR

THE BLACK EGGS

IN THE MIDDLE of the night we were awakened by one of those violent storms which can suddenly break out over the Caspian Sea. Lightning flashed across the sky and the wind howled. If the sea becomes too agitated we won't be able to go tomorrow, I thought unhappily, and fell asleep again.

But when the alarm clock shrilled at half-past four the storm had abated. A few minutes later Abdul and I were on our way through the dark, deserted streets of the little town. Chi-yun stayed behind. She is from the inland city of Peking, and saw the sea for the first time when she was sixteen. She has never quite overcome her fear of it.

The fishermen had said that under no circumstances would they leave before five o'clock, so I could hardly believe my eyes when we reached the harbour. All the little boats that had been there the day before were gone! One takes for granted that Persians are late, but that they should do anything *ahead* of time—this was something new to me.

Just then I caught sight of a boat at the end of the pier and ran to it. It was about fifteen feet long, flat-bottomed and had a short, thick mast.

I have been given warmer welcomes than the one I received when I jumped on board. The crew of four all shouted angrily, and one of the men even tried to push me ashore again.

"What's the big idea?" I shouted to Abdul, who had remained irresolutely on the pier. "First they try to sneak off without me, and now they want to throw me ashore!"

"Perhaps they would rather not have your company," Abdul suggested. "The thought had also occurred to me," I replied sarcastically, "but why don't they want me to go with them? After all, they said yesterday that I was very welcome to join them."

"Haven't you discovered that people don't always mean what they say?" Abdul asked. The fishermen now began assuring me that one risked one's life by going out just after a storm. The boat had no keel and could easily capsize. This had happened a couple of months ago, when three men lost their lives. (I later learned that the story was true except that it had happened more than a year ago and only one man was drowned.) It wasn't so dangerous for the fishermen, who were all good swimmers.

"So am I," I put in, whereupon they suddenly gave in—Persians often do so when an argument begins to tire them. But now Abdul began to complain that he was tired, and felt dizzy and unwell. When I paid no attention he declared that he could not swim.

"But yesterday you told me you could swim like a fish," I exclaimed. "Yes," he admitted reluctantly—"but only in shallow water." He had never been so far out that he could not touch bottom, and was suddenly convinced that then he would not be able to swim . . .

I did not hear any more, for the fishermen had pushed off and we were gliding out in the water. Abdul, who was still standing on the pier, soon disappeared in the darkness. With short, powerful strokes of the oars the fishermen rowed through the agitated water at the entrance of the harbour. Though the Caspian hardly contains any salt the waves were white-capped. A little distance from the shore the water became calmer.

The new day was beginning. Slowly the mountains that separate the humid Caspian region from the dry desert further south began to take shape. Ahead, the world's largest inland lake emerged from the vanishing night.

Only now could I discern the features of the four men who were pulling at the oars. The one who was closest to me was manipulating the tiller with his bare foot as he rowed. When they realized that I was watching them, they nodded to me and smiled. This surprised me, since they had just attempted to get rid of me. There must be something behind this whole thing which I did not understand.

Muscular legs stuck out from their ragged trousers which they had rolled up to the knees. From their gaunt, unshaven faces, beads of perspiration trickled down into the thick black matting or hair which many Persian men have on the chest. Three of them had wretchedly poor teeth.

Every half-hour or so they had to bale the leaky boat. It looked very old, full of cuts and gashes, and the oars were worn thin at the middle. Now I understood why the Persian sturgeon fishers stay close to land, although they are permitted to operate up to a distance of twenty miles from the shore. It was dangerous to go far out in the barge-like little vessels.

Their Russian competitors, who fish further to the north, have a fleet of fast motor-boats. No wonder that they catch the lion's share of the valuable fish.

The previous day we had visited the local caviar factory which is one of four or five situated on the southern shores of the Caspian. These state-owned factories export a total of about two hundred tons of caviar a year valued at about a million pounds sterling.

Most of it goes to the United States and Western Europe. The Russians buy the "poor" caviar which the Persians produce—that is to say, the roe which has been crushed inside the sturgeon during the fishing. Pressed, salted and dried, this caviar can keep much longer than first-class caviar and costs only about half as much.

The director of the factory had told us that there is also a considerable difference in the price of large and small eggs. The big ones cost about 40 per cent more, but only because of their appearance, for the taste is the same.

For some unknown reason, a few sturgeon have a golden roe which people mention almost with awe. It is called *royal* caviar and is by custom reserved for the Shah and his court. As far as we were concerned, the golden caviar lost some of its fascination when the director told us that it tastes exactly like the black.

Was it true that the delicious black roe make women more prolific and men more virile? The director smiled.

"I don't know from personal experience, but it is possible," he replied.

After a tour of the factory, we were given a spoon each and placed in front of a heaping platter of caviar. We were welcome to eat as much as we liked, the director said, and he didn't have to ask us twice. We have both been wild about caviar ever since our first taste of it in Rumania twenty years ago. It was relatively cheap there, as the sturgeon from which the caviar comes is also found in the brackish waters at the mouth of the Danube. But in those days we were very poor, so we never ate any except when we were invited to receptions or cocktail parties. Then you could always find us close to the dish with caviar canapés.

Since then, eating all the caviar we could had been our idea of the seventh heaven. However, after about a dozen mouthfuls of the glistening, slightly salty fish eggs, we both stopped and looked sadly at each other. We just couldn't get another mouthful down!

"Our visitors never eat very much caviar," the director told us with a slight smile. "It is much more filling than you think..."

The fishermen must have rowed for about an hour and a half, when we reached a long row of cork floats. That was the first of the fishing nets which we were to empty. There were three of them, each over a thousand feet long.

One of the fishermen went out in the stern, another placed himself behind him with a wooden club and a short boat-hook. The two others stayed at the oars, mainly to prevent the boat from rolling too much.

The man in the stern leaned out over the side and grabbed hold of the net, which hung a yard below the surface of the water, suspended between the cork discs and some stones fastened to the bottom. Slowly he pulled the boat alongside the net, his eyes peering into the murky water.

Suddenly he raised his arm. The man behind him hurried to his side and, with a quick movement, they jerked a big fish into the boat. It was about three feet long and had its fins entangled in the net. Even after a knock on the head with a heavy wooden club it continued to thrash its tail in an attempt to escape. The two men cursed as they fought to free its fins from the net. One of them grabbed the boat-hook and jabbed the point into the head of the fish. It gave a gasp, almost like a sigh, and then lay still.

Now it was easy to get it out of the net. One of the men made a slit in its belly with his pocket knife. No roe—it was a male. With wry faces they pushed it up in front of the mast.

The net had been badly torn, but the fishermen quickly repaired it, threw it out again, and we rowed on.

I sat down and looked at the dead fish. It reminded me a little of a shark, but instead of the fearful mouth of the tiger of the sea it had a kind of snout. I had heard that the sturgeon can become more than a hundred years old. How long had this one been allowed to live? It didn't look as if it could weigh more than a hundred pounds. Sturgeon of more than a thousand pounds have been caught, so this one must have been a youngster.

The man in the stern raised his arm once more and muttered something. His comrade jumped to his side. Again they began eagerly to pull the net on board; it must have been heavy for I could see the muscles in their backs tighten with the effort.

One of them gave a shout—undoubtedly an oath, for the fish had escaped from the net. The man in the stern raised the net and showed me a big hole torn by the fish. "Khub nist," he said. That was one Persian expression I had learned —*not good*. It must be the quality of the net he was referring to, for now he broke a couple of cords with the greatest of ease to show me how weak they were.

"Nylon khub," he added, and the others nodded. Yes, nylon was strong, but . . . He shrugged his shoulders. They were not given nylon nets.

The next sturgeon we caught was also a male, but a greyish mass oozed out of the third one when they cut open its belly. At last a female!

For the next four hours the men worked without stopping. The sun began to bake, so to prevent the fish from spoiling, a tarpaulin was thrown over them. The Persians are fond of the rather tasty flesh of the sturgeon, but it costs around ten shillings a pound, so few can afford it and most of it is exported to Russia.

When the last net had been inspected and repaired we had caught nine sturgeon, of which eight were males. On the return trip we hoisted a ragged sail and let the wind pull us while the men relaxed. When they talked it seemed to be mostly about money. Again and again I heard them mentioning figures followed by "toman".

As we were approaching the shore I could sense a change in their attitude towards me. They were talking about me, but avoided my eyes. Finally one of them took his pocket knife and cut open the belly of the female sturgeon. The greyish-black eggs that came spilling out had very little taste. That they only acquire after they have been rubbed gently through a sieve and salted slightly. After that they are ready to be tinned and exported.

I thought at first that the fishermen were removing the

roe just to help their comrades in the factory, but it soon dawned on me that their motives were not quite so noble, for they wrapped the quivering mass in a cloth and hid it carefully in the stern. The rest of the fish was thrown into the water, and finally they washed the blood away, sat down again, and looked questioningly at me. Was I going to tell on them? I smiled good-naturedly to show that I wasn't, but I must admit that I was a bit shocked.

When we entered the harbour the other boats had already returned. Abdul was waiting for me at the pier; if he felt any qualms at having deserted me in the morning his cheerful smile did not reveal it. We stood for a while and watched the fishermen carry their catch to the factory. Several of the others had not caught a single female sturgeon either—or so they said. Undoubtedly they too had some caviar hidden away.

But now I no longer felt shocked, for Abdul had told me what he had learned about the fishermen's lot. Their salary was about seven pounds a month. On top of that the men received a percentage of the catch equivalent to twopence for each pound of sturgeon and two shillings and sixpence for each pound of caviar. With luck, a fisherman could make fifteen pounds a month, but ten was more common.

That evening we sent Abdul to town to buy some caviar on the black market. He returned with a pound for which he had paid eleven shillings. He did not care to have any, but Chi-yun and I tried our best to polish it off, aided by a bottle of Persian vodka. We ate more and more slowly, until finally I put down my spoon.

" If herring cost as much as caviar," I said, " and caviar as little as herring—what do you think would taste better?"

"Fried herring," she replied without hesitation, but then that has always been one of her favourite dishes.

CHAPTER FIVE

TELL IT TO THE SHAH

IT DID NOT surprise me to hear that Taslimi had been a highwayman in his younger days. He looked exactly the part, and if it were still possible to practise this profession I'm sure he would do it.

He was seventy-seven years of age, but still bursting with life. We had met him through an acquaintance who was his doctor. The previous day we had arrived here in Gunbad Quabus, armed with a letter of introduction for the doctor, who received us with the usual Persian hospitality. When he asked us what we were interested in, we replied: Turkmenians—preferably former robbers.

That should not be very difficult, the doctor replied with a smile, for practically all the old Turkmenians who had survived the days of Reza Shah had been robbers. The first one who came to his mind was Taslimi.

He was a wealthy man, the owner of a village and two dwellings which lay in a dusty courtyard behind a high clay wall. One was an expensive two-storeyed villa, very modern. The other, which lay close by, was a round tent of the kind used by the nomadic Turkmenians.

Of course we were first invited inside the fine house. There were chairs and tables and a stack of expensive carpets in every room, but somehow we had a feeling that it had all been carried in from a removal van, dumped down in the most convenient spot and left there.

Taslimi's face brightened when we politely told him that we were much more interested in his Turkmenian house. Despite many years as a town dweller, he was not yet accustomed to living inside stone walls. Going down to the tent, we caught a glimpse of three women who were watching us curiously through a half-open door. They were his three wives. Two were old and wrinkled, the third looked as if she were no more than twenty.

In the semi-dark tent, Taslimi sat down on the carpet-covered floor, crossed his legs and heaved a sigh of contentment. That was so much better than a chair! The walls were made of thick brown felt stretched over a scaffold of poles which curved in at the top, leaving a hole in the centre through which the smoke could escape. There was no furniture, only a pile of rugs, a few utensils made of wood or iron, and some chests that looked very old.

A veiled serving-woman brought us tea. Taslimi emptied his glass noisily and then sucked his moustache dry. No, he did not mind telling us about the life of the Turkmenians in the old days. They had been bad times, with constant danger and barbaric customs. Today, with law and order in the land, everything was better.

I leaned closer towards the old man. "Wasn't it really more fun in the old days?" I asked. Taslimi's cunning little eyes blinked rapidly and a smile spread from the bearded mouth to the broad cheekbones.

"Sure, it was a wonderful life," he replied with feeling.

"You seldom knew how you were going to get your next meal, but you could always steal a camel and eat it, or go hunting."

The Turkmenians are one of the many wild nomadic peoples that have come charging out of Central Asia during the last two thousand years to knock at the gates of China, India, Persia and Europe. Some settled down in Finland, others in Hungary and Turkey.

The Turkmenians, who were among the last to come, chose the wide expanses east of the Caspian Sea. The dense forest then covering the area was ideal for hiding and digesting the loot between their plundering expeditions.

In those days Turkmenistan was divided between countless little tribes, each with its own chief, Taslimi told us. They were often at war with each other, either because a tribe had plundered a caravan within the domain of its neighbour, or because they had abducted each other's women.

A Turcoman with self-respect ought to have four wives, so naturally there are not enough women to go round. Of course one could buy a wife—one was simply forced to do so nowadays—but it was an expensive business. The price had hardly changed since Taslimi's youth. For a girl of good family, one still paid as much as for a good horse.

If a Turcoman loses his wife, custom demands that he pay twice as much for the next one. If the second wife also dies, the price is redoubled.

"So when a Turcoman's wife feels even slightly indisposed her husband immediately sends for me," the doctor said with a laugh. "They are my best patients."

Taslimi told us a story which he found highly amusing.

Once when he was a young man, a friend had offered to help a Persian merchant buy some sheep cheaply. The merchant wanted to see them first, so they rode to a Turkmenian camp outside the city. Taslimi's friend chatted with their hosts in their own language over a glass of tea. When he rose and left, the merchant got up to follow him, but was held back by the Turcomans.

"You have to stay here," they told the hapless Persian. "We have just bought you from him."

When Reza Shah came to power in the early twenties, the heyday of the Turcomans was over. He gave the robbers a chance to surrender and struck ruthlessly at those who didn't.

"I've been told that some of the leaders were thrown into boiling water," I interjected.

"That's not true!" Taslimi exclaimed indignantly. "No Turcoman was ever killed that way. But some were flayed alive," he added in a milder tone.

When highway robbery became too dangerous, the Turcomans had to find some other way of making a living, so they burned the great forests and began to till the soil. The ashes of the trees further enriched the fertile virgin soil, and Turkmenistan soon became the richest agricultural area in Persia, with cotton as its main produce.

The Shah kept a large part of the land for himself and leased it to tenant farmers. The rest was divided among the Turcomans whose chiefs naturally kept the lion's share. Aided by tractors, some of them became prosperous farmers, but the majority remained poverty-stricken share-croppers.

Shortly before the power of the Turcomans was broken,

Taslimi had fought his way up to become leader of a small band of robbers, so now he was a big farmer.

It would be a great pleasure, he said, to show us his village.

"Thanks," we replied politely, "but that would be too much trouble, and besides, the doctor has promised to drive us out in the country in his jeep." Taslimi wouldn't hear of this. Tomorrow morning he would come to fetch us in his car. Would seven o'clock suit us?

At the stroke of seven next morning we were in the lobby of our dirty little hotel. We were somewhat surprised when the doctor turned up. After all, Taslimi had promised to look after us, so there seemed no need for him to come along.

A quarter of an hour went by, half an hour, one hour. The doctor sat calmly in his chair and chatted with us. Now it began to dawn on us why he had come.

At nine we decided not to wait any longer, but just to make sure that there had not been a misunderstanding, we stopped at Taslimi's house on our way out of town. After all, he might have overslept, but the maid informed us that the master had gone out.

"That's the way they are," the doctor said with a shrug. "Charming and pleasant, but in a moment of enthusiasm they will promise you heaven and earth."

At first we drove on the asphalt strip running straight through the town. Along the main street there wasn't a single shop with windows, but there were bright Pepsi-Cola signs everywhere. The moment the asphalt ended we were hurled about in the jeep, and from then on we left a screen of dust behind us. On the right there were great mountains, to the left a plain stretched as far as the eye could reach. Over it hovered a light blue mist which gave it the appearance of the sea.

At intervals of a couple of miles, an earthen mound raised itself above the flat landscape. They reminded me a little of the ancient Vikings' burial grounds that are scattered throughout Scandinavia, only they were much larger. Nobody knows who built them. Some guess it was the Scythians, who ruled here long before the arrival of the Turcomans; others believe it was the Mongols.

Perhaps they served as signal towers at the time when the place was covered in forests. If an enemy approached it was possible to relay warnings with smoke signals. They may also have been graves. When one of the hills was excavated a few years ago, remains of utensils from about 5000 B.C. were found.

We followed a rough track running between gently rustling fields of cotton. The white flowers looked just like cotton balls decorating Christmas trees. The doctor showed us a field where the cotton plants grew thickly to a height of more than three feet.

"They have plenty of water here," he said.

He pointed at another field covered with puny shrubs of about ten inches. "There's no water over there."

When Persian farmers talk about "good" or "bad" soil, they really mean land with or without water. The life-giving liquid comes from the mountains in little rivulets, turning into shallow streams which are finally swallowed up by the thirsty earth. In most parts of Persia, hardly any rain falls, so the farmers are badly off if there are no mountain streams in the vicinity of their land.

We came to a cluster of wretched straw hovels which looked as if a gust of wind would send them tumbling. In front of them sat some ragged people who did not look in the least like the strong Turcomans; they were small and finely built, with curly hair and dark skin. " Baluchis," said the doctor.

We had heard about these refugees from the drought-stricken areas in Persian Baluchistan, hundreds of miles towards the south-east. It was the first time we had seen any of them, however, so we asked the doctor to stop for a moment.

They told us that for five years their farms back home had not yielded any crops from lack of rain. Finally they had sold what little they owned to get money for the journey here. The fields surrounding the little colony were leased to them by the Shah's sister, who owned vast tracts of land in Turkmenistan. They received three-fifths of the harvest—those were the usual terms in this part of the country. Usually tenants were also given a house to live in, but they had been told to build their own homes.

How much did their share of the harvest amount to in cash? In a good year a family could make 1500 tomans, that is about six pounds a month. In a bad year, they made much less.

We drove on towards the north, away from the mountains. Around noon we reached a long building with many doors. Some distance away, in front of a group of round Turkmenian huts, a horse was tethered. A thick felt blanket that had been wrapped around its body made it look strangely out of shape.

It is said of the Turcomans that they take better care of

their horses than of their children, the doctor told us. As nomads and as robbers, their lives had depended on the speed of their animals. Horse-breeding is still a lucrative business; a first-class Turkmenian horse fetches a couple of thousand pounds, and the fleetest make their careers on the racetracks of the capital.

The space immediately surrounding the dwellings was littered with refuse. Nomads are used to moving away from their garbage, so it does not even occur to them to remove it now that they have settled down. We were surrounded by bearded men wearing tall fur caps. It is said that the Turcomans even sleep with their fur caps on, but I forgot to ask about it.

We were invited for tea inside a spotlessly clean round-hut. The family possessions were put away in sacks or chests, a habit from former days when they had to be ready to break camp at a moment's notice.

These men now owned the land they tilled, but it had once belonged to the Shah, whose estates made up about one-tenth of all cultivated land in the country. Some years ago, however, he had begun to distribute it among the tenants.

We had read about this—what newspaper has not told about the Shah who gave his land to the poor? The distribution of the Shah's estates had been only the first step in the great land reform movement which had been going on for about two years. So far, one-fifth of the country has been affected by it.

"You must be much better off after the Shah gave you his land," I said to the farmers. They looked at me in surprise. "*Gave*?"

" Yes, he gave you the land, didn't he?"

" No, he most certainly did not," they replied in a chorus. They were paying for it—several hundred tomans a year for fifteen years.

Chi-yun and I looked questioningly at the doctor, who nodded. Yes, indeed, the farmers who took over the Shah's estates had to pay for the land. The Shah had received the entire sum immediately from the agricultural bank, which then had to collect it from the farmers over a period of fifteen years.

" Anyway, you are much better off now that you own the land, aren't you?"

" Better off?" They shook their heads. " No, we are worse off! "

" How is that possible? After all, you were tenant farmers before, and had to give a share of the harvest to the Shah. Now you don't have to do so."

" That's true, but we used to have better land, and much more of it."

One of the men told us that before the Shah sold his estates, he had rented a hundred acres. " My land was over there by the tree," he said, pointing through the door of the hut. There was no mistaking the spot, for on it grew the only tree within miles.

He had made a good living in those days, he continued. He had bought a steel plough and a tractor.

When the Shah sold his estates, no farmer had been permitted to buy more than ten acres. There was no choice of lots—they were sold poor land, salty and without water . . .

" Listen, there must be some mistake here," I broke in.

" You can't *all* have received poor land. What happened to the good land?"

It had been sold by the Shah's agents to rich townspeople, they replied. Most of the good land had been bought by officers and people who had the right connections. They did not cultivate the land themselves, but rented it out, mostly to refugees from Baluchistan.

" Now I cannot even go there any more," continued the man whose land lay around the lone tree. " It was my father who broke the soil. He improved the land and so did I. Now others are reaping the fruits of our labour."

One of the men fetched a jug of water and let us taste it. I spat it out, it was so salty. That was what came out of the wells here. It could not be used, not even for watering the fields, and they had to get their drinking water from an artesian well in the next village.

Their gloomy expressions disappeared when they heard that we were going to interview the Shah. " Tell him about us," they pleaded. " Tell the Shah that we have been unjustly treated."

When we drove away they waved to us: a small cluster of men in the wide, empty landscape. Then they disappeared in the dust from our jeep.

CHAPTER SIX

THE SACRED CITY

IN THE DINER of the train I ordered a beer. I should never have done so, for at once there was an icy silence.

Of course the "Pilgrim Express" was "dry", Abdul whispered to me. After all, Mohammed was a teetotaller!

As far as I know, Chi-yun and I were the only non-believers on the train. This had certain advantages. Several times a day—at the hours of prayer—we would get the compartment all to ourselves. Then all the believers would swarm out on the platform, each one carrying a prayer rug, though a few used a newspaper instead. They all knew in which direction to turn, for at every major station there was a signpost with an arrow and the word Mekka.

We were on our way to Mashhad, a town situated in the north-western corner of Persia, not far from the border of Afghanistan. Every year more than a million pilgrims go there.

Just looking out of the window was enough to make you thirsty. The heat seemed to shimmer above the bleak desert where all life appeared to have died out. You hardly dared to believe your own eyes when, at long intervals, a green spot would appear. Was it a mirage? No, the explanation was to be found in the underground canals—*quanats*—which brought water from distant mountains and made the desert bloom.

At dawn we were awakened by Abdul, who was trembling with excitement. He was born and raised in Mashhad, and had not seen his family since he left for Teheran two years ago to seek his fortune.

"We're almost there!" he said, and a moment later the holy city appeared in the sunrise. Floating on a sea of flat-roofed clay houses was a group of magnificent mosques with a golden-domed shrine in the centre. In this shrine rest the earthly remains of one of the most important of the many martyrs of the Persian Shia sect.

The Persians are individualists to an extreme, and some scholars of religion believe that their real purpose in founding the Shia sect was to make themselves less dependent on the Arabs. This was in the days when fanatical hordes from the Arabian desert had conquered Persia in the name of the new prophet. The helpless Persians were forced to acknowledge Allah as the one and only God. As far as the successors of the Prophet were concerned, however, they stubbornly refused to go along with the other Mohammedans, who supported one of the fathers-in-law of the deceased. Instead, they elected one of the Prophet's sons-in-law, Ali, and his descendants as their temporal leaders.

This led to bloody religious wars in which Ali and his line invariably came out as losers. One after the other of Ali's descendants, who all went by the title of *Imam*, was murdered by the Sunnis, as the other Mohammedans are called. The last Imam, who was number twelve, disappeared under mysterious circumstances 1120 years ago, but no Shia believes that he died. He is in hiding, they claim, and one day he will re-appear on a white charger with a sword in his hand and convert the whole world to the true faith . . .

I looked at the sparkling golden building where the fourth of the murdered Imams lies buried—all twelve have been granted sainthood. It was strictly prohibited for non-believers to enter, I knew. Only a year ago a German tourist had been knifed because he stepped inside the main gate to take a picture. Abdul and I had agreed that I would enter in disguise. Forbidden fruit always being more tempting, I was looking forward very much to doing this.

From the railway station a broad, tree-lined boulevard led to the centre of the city. Water streamed through open sewers—every morning at this time the sluices were opened so that the city could get rid of its garbage. The women looked like gliding tents, completely hidden beneath their long *chadurs*. The bearded mullahs were resplendent in their flowing, priestly robes and snow-white turbans. A few wore a green head-dress to show that they were *seyyids*, descendants of the Prophet. Few Persians will turn away a *seyyid* asking for alms, so they make a good living on charity.

In our democratic age it can seem unjust for such privileges to be inheritable, but Abdul assured us that there was no reason to pity the many beggars who had no right to wear the green. They came to Mashhad from all over the country to prey on the pilgrims, who are a soft touch because Mohammed specifically ordered his adherents to give alms to the poor. Some beggars were blind, others maimed, and those who could not arouse pity in any other way carried a sick child.

7. The mosaic work in Isfahan's mosques is regarded as the finest in the world. The majority of the many beautiful buildings in the city were built by Shah Abbas, about the time of Christian IV.

8. In a tea-house Isfahan, a passing minstrel tells of his country's history. He knows hundreds of verses by heart – and only now and again casts a sidelong glance towards the open book.

9. The carpet factory in Isfahan. One of the men "in charge" drinks a glass of tea during a break. He looks a good deal older than his 38 years.

10. This was once the entrance to the royal palace of Persepolis. The two animal sculptures with human faces show an Assyrian influence.

"They rent them," Abdul explained. "The sicker the children are, the higher the rent."

As soon as he had taken us to a hotel he rushed to his home, to return an hour later with a big smile on his face. His father had invited us for lunch! We were very much surprised, for Abdul had told us that his father, a deeply religious carpenter, shied away from all contact with foreigners, even indirectly. This had been quite troublesome for Abdul, who had been a tourist guide in Mashhad before he went to Teheran. Every time he went out with non-Mohammedan tourists, his father had insisted on his going to a bath-house before he was permitted to enter his home.

Altogether, his father seemed to have become more tolerant during his son's absence. Abdul was no longer required to take a bath when he had been with non-believers—it was enough for him to wash his hands, his father had told him.

I had a feeling that Abdul was a little embarrassed to show us how poor his family was. They lived in one room in a shabby compound—father, mother, a fourteen-year-old sister and two smaller brothers. Abdul's mother and sister served us tea as we sat with folded legs on a threadbare rug. All we could see of them was their hands and feet and a sparkling eye that peeped at us from the folds of the *chadur*.

His father, a slight, greying man in shirtsleeves, sat by himself, apparently a little disconcerted by the whole situation. This was not surprising, for he had just touched an infidel for the first time in his life. When Abdul introduced us to him, I had thoughtlessly held out my hand instead of bowing. He gave a start, but could not very well refuse to take it. It was the most unresponsive hand I had ever shaken.

After tea, plates of food were set on a colourful piece of plastic laid on the floor. It took some time to chew the tough roast mutton. Afterwards we were served a tasty vegetable soup with bread broken into it.

During the meal, Abdul's mother and his sister Reseta sat at a distance from us, inscrutable behind their *chadurs*. On his arrival, Abdul had learned that Reseta was going to get married in ten days. It was forbidden for girls under sixteen to marry, but many did so, he told us. Thus, one of their neighbours had married his daughter off when she was only thirteen. It was expensive to have a grown-up girl at home, and it was also risky.

Their future son-in-law, a thirty-year-old house painter, had heard about Reseta from a professional matchmaker. He had to pay Abdul's father six hundred tomans, and nobody likes to buy a pig in the poke, so he had been permitted to see her once without a veil on. She had walked rapidly through the room where he sat, closely guarded by his future father-in-law. This glimpse had convinced him that she was worth the money.

" What if Reseta had not cared for him?" Chi-yun asked.

" Her opinion was not taken into consideration," Abdul replied, " and anyway she will probably be happy if only to get away from home.

" Father took her out of school when she was ten," he explained. She had wept, for she wanted very much to go on studying, but he was adamant. It was improper for such a big girl to be taught by male teachers, he maintained. Since then she had been a virtual prisoner—she was not allowed to go out except in the company of her parents or another adult, and then of course she had to wear her *chadur*.

Chi-yun wanted to ask Reseta and her mother how they liked wearing the *chadur*, but Abdul shrugged his shoulders. "What's the use? In Father's presence they won't say what they think, anyway," he said, adding that they had probably never even asked themselves whether they liked to wear the *chadur*. It was something one had to do, so why speculate about it? In Teheran one often saw unveiled women, but seldom in the small towns or in the countryside. Here in Mashhad, girls began wearing the *chadur* at the age of six.

At one time the *chadur* had been strictly prohibited in Persia. That was during the reign of the present king's father, the great Reza Shah. The mullahs were furious when he ordered the arrest of all women who wore veils in public. The Koran does not specifically command women to wear veils, but it had gradually become a custom.

The mullahs had decided to fight the new law with all means at their disposal. One cannot help admiring their courage, for no one had thus far succeeded in standing up against Reza Shah. From all over the country the defiant mullahs went to Mashhad, where they gathered in a courtyard adjacent to the golden shrine. There were between two and three thousand of them, and they unanimously condemned the new law, and urged the women of Persia not to obey it.

The Shah ordered them to go home and refrain from discussing the matter. This they refused to do, and, since nothing happened right away, some of them may have believed that the Shah was wavering, that perhaps he would finally give in.

Late the following night, the shrine area was quietly surrounded by soldiers. Machine-guns were placed on the roofs around the courtyard where the mullahs were conducting their sit-down strike. The gates were closed, and for several minutes the staccato barking of the machine-guns could be heard in the city. During the rest of the night, military trucks rumbled through the streets with the dead—Abdul's father remembered it clearly.

"You can still see the bullet holes in the marble walls of the courtyard," Abdul said. "I'll show you tomorrow when we visit the shrine."

From that day on the veil was no longer seen in Persia, but it reappeared during the last war, when the country was occupied by the Allies. They had forced the dictatorial Reza Shah to abdicate in favour of his son, and the people soon discovered that now they could violate many of the old Shah's laws with impunity. Reza Shah had succeeded in making the Persians obey, but not in changing their way of thinking . . .

We rose and took leave of our host, for our knees had begun to ache from the unaccustomed position. I pointed at the plates which Abdul's mother was picking up and asked jokingly whether they had to be cleaned specially carefully because we had used them.

"Yes, they have to be rinsed three times because you are non-believers," he replied. As if to console us, he added with a laugh: "If a dog has licked a plate it has to be rinsed seven times!"

We had decided to visit the golden shrine on the afternoon of the following day, and in the morning Abdul and I went to reconnoitre the area. The bazaar around the holy buildings was swarming with people. Pedlars advertised their wares in raucous voices and from the street kitchens came a redolent smell of roast lamb. A heavily laden mule raised its muzzle and brayed heart-rendingly.

" I think we had better not go any closer," Abdul said when we reached a gate leading to a great courtyard in front of a mosque. Behind the onion-shaped cupola rose the golden shrine, magnificent against the blue sky.

" That was where the German tourist was knifed," Abdul continued, pointing through the gate and adding something about being careful. I was not listening, for I had just spotted what seemed to be an excellent subject for a picture, and was busy focusing.

Suddenly I was pushed violently from behind and someone hit me in the neck so that I reeled. With the speed of lightning, a crowd had gathered around me, their fists raised threateningly. Abdul, after some fast talking, succeeded in dissuading them from taking further punitive action and we walked away quickly, followed by their curses.

" I'm not sure it will be wise to go to the shrine, even in disguise," Abdul said thoughtfully. It was beginning to dawn on him that he might also suffer if I were caught.

There really wasn't much to see anyway, he continued—just a lot of pilgrims and mullahs, and also some prostitutes who went under another name. *Sigheh,* or temporary mates, they were called. Even if a man had four wives at home, he could take over a *sigheh* without troubling his conscience—of course against a suitable fee. The contract, which had to be signed by a mullah, specified how long the union was to last. Sometimes it was only a matter of hours, but it could also be for several months, or even years.

Someone lay buried under each tile in the golden shrine, Abdul continued. The closer the grave was to the marble sepulchre of the sacred Imam, the more it cost. He had heard of families who had paid up to 100,000 tomans to secure a good place.

When he was a boy, his father had often taken him to the golden shrine during the month of fasting. He had hated being pushed about in the milling throng of pilgrims whom the mullahs drove to a frenzy with their rantings about how the holy Imams had died as martyrs. All the male pilgrims had bare torsos, and shouted in ecstacy as they struck themselves violently on the chest with clenched fists. They did it in unison, so you could hear the hollow thumping from a great distance. Some would also hit themselves on the forehead, just below the hairline, with the blade of a sword. When a big bump appeared they would slash it so the blood came spurting out . . .

"Ugh!" Abdul shook his head as if to get rid of the thought. "It used to give me nightmares—I don't think God really likes such things."

As I listened to Abdul, a struggle was taking place within myself. One voice urged me to go ahead with my plan of visiting the golden shrine in disguise. "Don't be a sissy," it said, but the next moment I would see the vengeful faces of the men who had attacked me outside the shrine. At that moment I had an inkling of the horror experienced by all those poor wretches who have been torn to pieces by howling mobs. Running such a risk hardly seemed worth while for the sake of seeing an old coffin.

I was finally saved from my dilemma, for early in the afternoon a volley of shots was fired somewhere in the city.

I did not even hear it, but a while later, the town was buzzing with rumours. The police had clashed with an angry mob, and several people had been hurt.

Most likely the mullahs had excited the people, Abdul said—exactly like the time when Reza Shah had banished the veil, only now it was something else they were demonstrating against. The Shah wanted to give the women of Persia the right to vote.

And behind this was another and much more important reason, Abdul continued. The Shah had also threatened to tax the religious institutions which own close to one-fifth of all the cultivated land in the country. If this was done, the mullahs would lose a huge source of income which was the true foundation of their power. In the hope of frightening the Shah, the mullahs were trying to put the people up against him.

With tension running high after the shooting, I felt better about letting Abdul persuade me to give up my plan. I think we were equally relieved, but he soon got something else to worry about. If I couldn't find something interesting to write about in Mashhad I would have to leave, I said—and he wanted so much to stay for his sister's wedding.

After numerous suggestions which did not find favour in my eyes he happened to mention an old acquaintance of his family, a fortune-teller who was an opium addict. I pricked up my ears. I had always wanted to try smoking opium. Perhaps this was my chance.

For days Abdul conducted secret negotiations. Finally—and strangely enough just the day before his sister was to get married—the fortune-teller agreed that I could come to his home for a pipe of opium.

The old man lived in a wretched hole in the bazaar district. His sallow complexion and incredible skinniness clearly revealed his addiction. For the sake of appearances he began by telling me my fortune. Among many other bright prospects for my future he mentioned that I would soon be going on a long journey, but he did not really have to be a fortune-teller to predict this. After all, I had to get back home from Persia.

Though he protested vehemently, I finally persuaded him to accept twenty tomans for his prophecies. This was what we had agreed I should pay for smoking opium.

I had never seen an opium pipe like the one he now took out from a hiding-place underneath the worn rug. It was only about ten inches long and ended in a round porcelain head with a tiny hole on top. Placing a little opium here, he held it over a charcoal fire until it burst into flame. He then handed me the pipe, telling me to suck vigorously and persistently.

I inhaled the nauseating smoke until I began to turn green in the face. The old man sniffed the fumes hungrily, his hands trembling. Hardly had the first lump of opium gone up in smoke, before he began preparing another. When I had smoked it too, he looked at me questioningly. Could I feel anything?

I shook my head, so he gave me another pipe, then another, and then a fifth. When I still could not feel anything the old man shrugged his shoulders regretfully. He did not think it worth while to expend any more opium on someone who was immune to it.

He himself had smoked from his early youth, he told me. In those days it had hardly cost anything, and there had been innumerable addicts. Now, almost the only opium smokers were old people.

I knew that until ten years ago there had been more than a million opium addicts in Persia. How admirable of the government to have defeated the evil in such a relatively short time, I thought, but then the old fellow remarked that the young people had switched to heroin. This is a derivative of opium, but much more powerful.

"And *that* is dangerous," he said. He could keep his opium consumption down to about a dozen pipes a day, but people who became addicted to heroin knew no moderation. Opium had become outrageously expensive, however, so he had to work harder at his fortune-telling to earn enough for his daily ration.

When we left, the world wasn't quite what it used to be. Everything was a little vague, and I suddenly decided to take a car home—something I ordinarily wouldn't dream of doing when it is only a matter of a short walk.

Chi-yun looked at me with wide-open eyes when I entered the hotel room. "What's the matter, Karl?" she asked. "You look so strange—what are you grinning at?"

"At myself," I replied. "Remember how unhappy I was because I couldn't go to that lousy shrine? Ridiculous to take it so seriously, wasn't it? Such things don't matter—the only thing that really matters is that one is happy."

The delayed intoxication lasted until way into the night. It was very pleasant, with a relaxed, strangely sweet feeling in the body, but since that day I have not felt the slightest desire to smoke opium again. For people like me, who have an aggressive nature, it is much more fun to take up the problems and fight them out rather than to push them aside with the help of opium.

I am not quite sure whether my wife also looks at it like that. " You were so sweet and pleasant that evening when you had smoked opium," she has told me several times with, it seems to me, a hint of nostalgia in her voice—but surely that must just be my imagination?

CHAPTER SEVEN

BAHA'I

THERE IS NO telling what can put you on the track of a story. I remember for instance the time when Abdul stopped drinking Pepsi-Cola. He was quite addicted to it, but stopped drinking it the moment we arrived at Mashhad. We wondered why, and finally we asked him.

Because the mullahs in Mashhad had declared holy war against Pepsi, he replied. At first we wouldn't believe him, but it turned out to be quite true. The mullahs had indeed excommunicated Pepsi-Cola! I then thought that this was prompted by the fear of imperialistic " coca-colonization ", but no, it was solely for religious reasons. The Mohammedans hated the director of the Pepsi-Cola plant because he was a Baha'i.

On our trips through Persia we had already met several followers of this faith. They had, without exception, turned out to be extremely punctual and straight-forward people—qualities one notices in Persia. But could it be for this reason that the mullahs hated them?

No, the director of the Pepsi-Cola plant replied when we looked him up the following day. The hatred of the mullahs was based on fear of losing supporters. Here in Mashhad alone, hundreds of Mohammedans went over to the Baha'i faith every year, and the same thing was happening all over the country.

" Not that we make any effort to convert people," he continued. " We have no missionaries, hold no revival meetings or anything like that. It isn't necessary. The young people come to us by themselves when they hear of the Baha'i message."

" What is this message?" I aked.

" The unity of man," he replied simply. " But I am not very good at explaining such things. Better come to our next evening meeting and learn for yourself. . ."

We thanked him, and one evening a few days later he came to fetch us, accompanied by his wife and two teenage daughters.

" Poor girls! " I exclaimed when I heard that they were going with us. The director replied that they liked to go to the meetings. The girls, who spoke some English, nodded eagerly and declared that they really enjoyed the evening gatherings tremendously.

" It's more fun than going to the movies," one of them added.

The street lamps of Mashhad shed about as much light as glow-worms, so many people carry a torch at night to avoid falling into the open sewers. In the darkness we could see hundreds of lights moving about. Most of them were Baha'is going to evening services, the director told us.

" But how many Baha'is are there in this town?"

" Over four thousand."

We could hardly believe our own ears, for Mashhad is

the stronghold of the Shia sect. Did the Baha'is really have a church large enough to seat so many? No, they did not use a church, but met in small groups in each other's homes . . .

A few minutes later we entered a very ordinary middle-class home, with steel-legged furniture, glass-topped tables and gaudy vases with plastic flowers set on embroidered table centres. A large number of people had gathered in the sitting-room. Some were dressed according to the latest European fashion, others wore the simple, loose garments of the Persian peasant. Conversation died away when a young girl rose and began to chant softly. Lips moved soundlessly, it seemed that everyone knew the words.

> Oh my Lord, oh my Lord,
> This is a lamp lighted
> By the fire of Thy love,
> And ablaze with the flame
> Which is ignited in the tree of Thy mercy.

Abdul gave us a whispered translation of the song. He seemed uneasy, and no wonder. Just to be here was a great sin for him, for to the Shias the Baha'is are the arch-enemy. At the same time he was probably looking forward to seeing all sorts of bad things, for it was whispered that the Baha'is smoked and drank and were promiscuous at their gatherings.

A grey-haired lady now read aloud from a book for a few minutes, and then spoke briefly on the bringing up of children. The young people in the gathering frequently broke in with questions or to state their points of view. Abdul's eyes widened as he heard girls of his sister's age express ideas that must have seemed revolutionary to him.

The paramount rule in bringing up children was to teach them to be honest, he translated for us. If a man had a son and a daughter, but could afford to send only one of them to school, he should send his daughter, as her influence was much more important than the son's in bringing up the next generation. A Mohammedan has only to state three times in public that he does not want his wife any more, then he is rid of her, but under Baha'i law it was as difficult for a man as for a woman to get a divorce. Young Baha'is chose their own spouses, but had to get their parents' permission to marry. The Baha'i movement approved of ballroom dancing—even the Twist—but prohibited its members from taking intoxicating drinks.

After the discussion and more tea, we persuaded the doctor's wife to tell us about the origin of " the new world faith ", as she called Baha'i. The others must have known the story by heart, yet they listened eagerly.

One day in the year 1844, a Mohammedan preacher arrived at Shiraz, a large oasis town in southern Persia. In front of the city gate he struck up conversation with a young business man, Ali Mohammed, who was liked by everyone for his kindness and generosity. They went to Ali's home, and here the preacher revealed that he was searching for a new prophet whose coming was predicted in the Koran. The prophet would be recognized by his ability to explain some moot points in the Koran.

What were these points? Ali Mohammed asked. When the difficult sentences were read aloud to him, he explained them with the greatest of ease.

"How do you know these things?" the mullah asked. Ali Mohammed had no idea. It was as if someone was speaking through his mouth, he said.

The mullah put his hand on Ali Mohammed's shoulder. "My search is over," he said. "You are the prophet."

After a moment of silence, Ali Mohammed shook his head. His task was only to prepare the way for someone else. When this was done, the true prophet would come.

"This will happen shortly after my death," he said.

The next day Ali Mohammed announced that he was the *Bab*—that is to say the Gate through which a new prophet would come. In the hope of making him a laughing stock, some mullahs who were present challenged him to a theological debate, but they came out second best from the encounter. Again and again he silenced them with his sagacious replies. He did not go against any of the Mohammedan dogmas, but asked for social justice and equal rights for women . . .

His words made a deep impression on the onlookers. Then as now, Persia was one of the most under-developed countries in the world, and many felt that a regenerator was sorely needed. The mullahs laughed contemptuously and accused him of being a swindler. They realized that the Bab could became a threat to their power, and some time later they succeeded in having him banished from Shiraz.

He went to Isfahan, where his message was received with enthusiasm. In a short time he had won thousands of adherents. Some were so inspired by him that they left their homes to follow the new leader.

The enemies of the Bab accused him of conspiring to

overthrow the Shah and mount the peacock throne himself. A disciple of the new prophet made an unsuccessful attempt on the life of the Shah, and this led to bloody reprisals against the entire movement. The Bab was imprisoned, and seven of his most faithful disciples were seized and brought before the prime minister. Outside the gate stood an executioner with a broadsword. They were told that they could save their lives by admitting that the Bab was a false prophet.

All seven chose death rather than deny their leader. The Bab's followers were now outlawed, and throughout the country the mullahs set the people against them. Several thousand died as martyrs—something one would not expect of the worldly Persians if they could possibly avoid it.

The Bab was condemned to death. During his last hours in prison he was dictating continuously to a secretary—there was still so much he wanted to explain to his followers. When the soldiers came to fetch him he asked them to give him time to finish, but at the order of an officer they grabbed him and dragged him to a large square in front of the prison. A rope was tied around his wrists, and, arms raised above his head, he was hoisted up in front of a wall. Some soldiers marched up and took aim.

"Fire!" There was a deafening roar, and the whole square was enveloped in smoke. When it drifted away, a shout rose from the crowd which had gathered to watch the execution. The Bab had disappeared.

"A miracle!" I exclaimed in disgust. It seems impossible to find a single religion which does not make use of the supernatural.

"No," the grey-haired lady said with a smile. There were

no miracles in Baha'i, and the Bab's disappearance must of course have its natural explanation. Perhaps the soldiers had felt it was wrong to kill him, so each one had aimed above his head, thus shattering the rope by which he was hanging. Under cover of the smoke he could then have picked himself up and walked back to his cell. That was where he was found a moment later, busily dictating. When they came again to take him to the execution grounds, he rose with a smile. Now he was ready, he said.

His disciples mourned him deeply, but kept up their spirits, for he had promised them that his successor would soon appear. Throughout Persia, small groups of people waited anxiously.

One of the Bab's followers was a tall, bearded man of good education. He was also condemned to death, but at the last moment was exiled to Baghdad instead. There he left his family, and for the next two years wandered about as a dervish.

Returning to Baghdad, emaciated and with his hair hanging down to his shoulders, he gathered those of the Bab's followers who had fled to this city. God had first spoken through the Bab, he told them, but in his wanderings he had become convinced that now he was the mouthpiece of the Almighty.

"I am the new prophet," he said quietly, and the others bowed their heads, knowing instinctively it was true. Baha'u'llah, they called him from that day—the Splendour of God.

The news soon spread to Persia that the Bab's successor had revealed himself. There were celebrations in thousands of homes. When the mullahs realized that the movement had not died out—that, on the contrary, persecution had strengthened it—they again went to the Shah. The new prophet was even more dangerous than the Bab, they said. The Shah believed them and persuaded the Sultan of Turkey to send Baha'u'llah even further away from Persia, to a small town in Palestine.

Here he stayed for the next ten years, at first in a dungeon with murderers and robbers. Some of his followers came all the way from Persia, but were not permitted even to see him, so they just stood silently outside the part of the building where they knew he was imprisoned.

His guards wondered about the middle-aged Persian. Though obviously a man of good family, he cheerfully ate the wretched food and comforted his fellow prisoners.

Soon the guards began to smuggle paper and ink to him, and in the dungeon he wrote several books which have later been translated into many languages.

Here the grey-haired lady put her hand on the book from which she had read aloud earlier in the evening. " Glimpses of Baha'u'llah's Teachings ", it was called. Though only a summary of his works, it was nearly four hundred pages long. She now read us a few samples of what it contained. Poor Abdul had a terrible time translating the poetic, flowery language used in those days.

It was indeed as if a higher power had revealed glimpses of the future to Baha'u'llah. A hundred years ago he described the world that was to come—the growth of nationalism, the world wars, the United Nations, even the exploitation of atomic energy. Again and again he emphasized that all humanity worships the same God. Zarathustra, Moses, Jesus, Mohammed—all were mouthpieces of the one and only God, and each one had fulfilled an important mission.

A world religion, the doctor's wife had said. Did she expect that one day all men would embrace Baha'i?

"Yes," she replied without hesitation. "Today, people everywhere are getting further and further away from God. They no longer believe in the divine order that lies behind everything. The religions have lost their appeal and cannot bring people back to God. Only we can, for our religion is the only one that has kept pace with the development of man. The old religions suited their times, but they have little to offer us now, steeped as they are in prejudices and dogmas."

As examples she mentioned that Mohammedans will not eat with non-Mohammedans, Hindus approve of the caste system, Christians split hairs over irrelevant dogmas and resist new ideas. All this, as Baha'u'llah had taught them, stood in the way of the unity of man.

"Won't Baha'u'llah's teachings also become obsolete one day?" I asked.

"Of course. Baha'u'llah wrote that when our religion becomes outdated, a new prophet will appear. And it will go on like this for ever. When man lives in accordance with the wishes of God, the possibilities for his development are unlimited. What these wishes are, the prophets reveal to us from time to time."

How many Baha'is were there? It was difficult to give an accurate answer, as the number was growing day by day. In Persia alone there were over half a million. Thousands of Persian Baha'is have migrated to foreign countries and, when requested by their friends, have told about the new message. These friends have again passed the word on to others. In underdeveloped countries, where people are searching for a new pattern of life, the progress of Baha'is has been especially impressive. Entire villages in India and Africa have gone over to the new faith. Today there are probably more Baha'is outside Persia than inside. One of the largest congregations is in the United States.

We were mistaken if we thought that it was easy to become a Baha'i. Just to say that you believe is not enough. You have to prove to a gathering of Baha'is that you truly understand the teachings of Baha'u'llah. Time and again the prophet said that it is wrong to accept an idea without weighing it thoroughly. Man should not let himself be guided by his emotions alone. He must use reasoning too.

Baha'u'llah recommended an annual fast of one month like the Mohammedans, but not just for religious reasons. It is good for the health and also serves to strengthen one's will-power, he said. He ordered his followers to engage in useful occupations and to obey the laws of their country, but forbade them to take active part in politics. All Baha'is obey this commandment, yet they have been persecuted time and again in Persia. Over twenty thousand have been killed since the Bab proclaimed his message. The mullahs use every opportunity to put the people up against the Baha'is, and formerly the authorities did nothing to protect them.

"But that has changed," the lady told us. During the last wave of persecutions nearly ten years ago, protests streamed in from Baha'i organizations throughout the world. In one day the Shah received over seven thousand telegrams. Then he ordered the police to stop the attacks.

The group around us nodded and smiled. They were

no longer alone, they belonged to a world-wide family.

Baha'u'llah also left rules for the organizing of the Baha'i movement. Whenever there are nine believers, a council is formed. Once a year, representatives from all over the country meet and elect a national council, also composed of nine. Above the national councils is a world council, likewise with nine members. One of them is an American negro.

We suddenly discovered that it was midnight, and after a last glass of tea, the meeting broke up. Everybody wanted to shake hands with us. Returning to our hotel, we again saw countless lights moving through the sleeping city beneath the silhouettes of the minarets.

CHAPTER EIGHT

ONLY ON FRIDAYS

MOHAMMED JERANGI IS one of the bearded dervishes who wander about in the Middle East with a begging bowl in their hand. There used to be thousands of them on the highways of Persia, but they don't seem to thrive in our busy, practical times. Today only a few hundred are left.

Abdul found him at a hostelry for holy men and persuaded him to come to our hotel. Instead of the remote, ascetic mystic Chi-yun and I expected to see, a vigorous young giant entered our room and looked at us with sparkling eyes. His long hair was tied up in a knot at the back of his head. He wore a faded blue jacket over a long robe that had once been white and held a staff and a huge begging bowl in his hand.

"Yah Ali!" he boomed; this means "Praise be to Ali!" and is often used as a greeting in the Shia sect. There were no chairs in our room, so Chi-yun and I sat on the bed while Mohammed Jerangi and Abdul settled down on the floor with their legs crossed. We learned that our guest came from Kerman, an ancient town in the south-eastern part of the country. His father had also been a dervish, and he himself had been on the road for most of his forty-four years.

Forty-four! I gave a start. I had just passed my forty-fifth birthday, but looked at least ten years older than Mohammed Jerangi. He seemed to have chosen a profession that kept one young.

" What is the difference between the Shias and the other Mohammedans?" I asked; " that is, apart from the fundamental disagreement about who are the true heirs of the Prophet?"

" We wash ourselves in different ways before we pray," Mohammed Jerangi replied. He showed us how the Shias let the water run from the elbow down over the hands, while the others let it run from the hands down to the elbow.

" In nature, water always runs downward, so our way is obviously the correct one," he continued earnestly. I found it hard to keep from smiling, but then I remembered the practices of other religious sects. Should one be sprinkled with holy water or not? Is a complete ducking necessary at baptism, or is it enough to pour a little water on the head?

" Do you really find it so important how you rinse your hands?" I asked. The sun-tanned dervish glanced quickly at me. It seemed to me there was a trace of a smile on his face, but it was hard to tell what was going on behind the big black beard.

" For some," he replied. " Each one finds his own way."

Those words seemed to have a familiar ring. Yes, of course! It was our good old Danish proverb: " Every man finds his own way to bliss."

" What is your way?" I continued. It is not an easy question to have flung at you by a stranger, but Mohammed Jerangi did not hesitate for a second.

"I seek God," he replied.

"I suppose we all do, but how do you seek God?"

Suddenly he tossed his head back with great force, then around and forward, and back again, around and around, faster and faster, at the same time shouting: "Yah Ali, yah Ali, yah Ali . . ." until the whites of his eyes showed. I could easily imagine that one could bring about a religious ecstasy in this way. When he stopped there were specks of froth at the corners of his mouth.

"I do that a thousand times," he said. "Then I am closer to God. But only on Fridays."

I chuckled at the last remark, although it did occur to me that we Christians also reserve one day in the week for God.

"When did you begin to wander?"

"I have always wandered—except during the time of Reza Shah . . ."

The great Shah, who almost single-handedly pulled Persia out of the dark Middle Ages, had outlawed the dervish profession as useless and harmful. Mohammed Jerangi became a cobbler, and for eight years he repaired shoes. He made good money and had been quite fond of the work, but as soon as the laws were relaxed after the young Shah came on the throne, he struck the road again. When we asked him why, he turned and looked out of the window.

"I feel closer to God when I move about," he replied. "For me it is easier to feel his presence when I am not occupied with practical matters. When I repair shoes, I think of the shoes."

Chi-yun wanted to know if it was true that dervishes were permitted to marry. Yes, they could have up to four wives,

Mohammed Jerangi replied, but few could afford even one. It was expensive to have a wife, and took a great deal of one's time.

"Time," I exclaimed. "But you have nothing but time!"

"Work is not the only thing a man can do," he replied with dignity. "Some find happiness that way, but what I do is more important to me."

I could imagine how people would greet such a remark in northern Europe. Lazy and anti-social, they would call him. The Oriental, who does not believe in our creed that work ennobles man, meets little understanding in our part of the world.

"Is it easy to make a living by begging?"

"I do not beg," Mohammed Jerangi replied without a trace of annoyance at the rather blunt question. "I help people, and if they want to they give me something in return."

How did he help people?

In a box which he had left in the lobby he kept a snake. If we wanted him to he would be glad to fetch it and show us how he could make it dance when he blew on his flute. People liked very much to watch this. Afterwards he would tell them about how happy God had made him. He would explain that the more you succeed in mastering your desire for material things, the closer you come to God . . .

I suddenly remembered the words from the Bible: "It is easier for a camel to pass through the needle's eye . . ." One seems to find this idea in all religions.

Not everyone understood him, Mohammed Jerangi continued, but most people would give him a mite, although it did not always add up to much. He had often gone hungry for days because he had no money for food. "But it is good for you to fast," he said. "And afterwards, food tastes even better."

"Remember how you jerked your head a while ago?" I asked and tried to imitate the movement—a bit too violently, for I almost sprained my neck. Mohammed nodded and made a few throws with his head. Yah Ali, yah Ali—that was the way to do it.

"Can't you contact God in some other way?" I asked.

The bearded dervish smiled. "What does it matter how you do it?" he asked. "God is everywhere. The important thing is that you search for him. You are bound to find him if you seek . . ."

He rose and put his palms together in front of his chest. "Yah Ali!" he said, indicating with a slight bow that if we wished to we could terminate the conversation. Before he left I gave him ten tomans. He was not used to getting so much, but I felt that I had had the better part of the bargain.

CHAPTER NINE

THE OLD CHILDREN

FOR EIGHT HOURS the bus from Teheran speeds southwards over a stony desert. Then Isfahan appears with its turquoise cupolas and minarets outlined against the azure sky. Along the main street, slender poplars stand guard between rows of low mud buildings. Even the slightest breath of wind makes the leaves rustle and glitter like silver.

If you turn down one of the narrow, dusty side streets you will soon hear sing-song voices coming from an open door. The sight that meets you if you step inside will remain for ever in your memory.

The picture is hazy at first, for the air in the huge, barn-like room is alive with fluffy particles. Little figures, all hunched up, perch on high scaffolds. They are the children who weave the famous carpets of Isfahan. Among them sit men who call out the colours that are used. " Two yellow threads, two reds, a yellow . . ." they chant. With lightning speed the little hands find the right thread, tie a knot, cut the thread . . .

A tremendous sneeze escaped me, for the fluffs of wool had tickled me in the nose. The children automatically turn their heads towards the noise, and the men calling out the colours grew silent as everybody stared at the two strangers who had entered the rug factory unannounced.

"*Salaam!*" I greeted them loudly, and a murmuring answer ran down the rows: "*Salaam.*" Then the men resumed the monotonous calls and the pale faces turned back reluctantly to the rugs. Now the director, a sallow man in a business suit, came towards us.

"What can I do for you?" he inquired politely, but I had a feeling that he would rather have seen our heels. Hearing that I was a journalist and wanted to do a story on a rug factory, he quickly began to explain that the children did not work here at all. In fact, not a single child was employed at his factory. They were just permitted to stay here because their mothers did not have time to look after them. To keep them from getting into mischief he allowed them to play with the looms.

"Of course he knows that we know this is nonsense," Abdul added. "But it is forbidden to employ children, so he has to say it."

The director readily consented when I asked for permission to take pictures of the children. Somehow I felt ashamed as I walked among them in search of the one that would most vividly illustrate their misery. I picked a lovely little girl with a kerchief around her head and a ragged sweater over her long cotton dress. She was seven years old and her name was Ishia.

I did not feel like questioning her further with the director standing next to me, so I asked Abdul to inquire whether it would be all right for us to accompany the little girl home at closing time and see how she lived. He would ask her father when he brought her lunch, replied the man who called out the colours at Ishia's rug.

"When does the factory close?" I asked.

"At seven o'clock in the evening."

"And what time do you open in the morning?"

"At six."

I thought I had misunderstood him, but Abdul assured me that a thirteen-hour workday was common at the rug factories. The wages varied from half a toman a day for the smallest childen to five tomans for adults...

This tore the director's kindergarten story to shreds, but he did not bat an eye. A senseless law had forced him to tell an obvious lie, but he was not going to make himself ridiculous by pretending to believe in the lie. We thanked him for his kindness and said we would return shortly before seven.

The rest of the morning Abdul and I spent in one of Isfahan's many tea-houses. *Kafekhanas,* or coffee saloons, they are called although nothing is served but tea. Until about a hundred years ago the Persians drank only coffee. Then, through contact with the Russians and the British, they were converted to tea, but the public houses have retained their name.

These *kafekhanas* are the gathering place for the men. Here they sit for hours on rugs spread over wooden benches or raised platforms of clay. The hubble-bubble goes from hand to hand; some bring their own mouthpiece, others use the public one. A man sings in a shrill, vibrating voice on the radio. The words may be different, but the way of singing is the same all the way from Delhia to Cairo and Casablanca, and even up to Spain.

The similiarity is not accidental. It was here in Persia that the Arabs in the seventh century had their first contact with an old culture. What they learned followed in the wake of their conquering armies. The fountains and arcades of the Alhambra in Spain, the philosophy and mathematics of Al-Azhar university in Cairo, the mosaic-ornamented palaces of Baghdad, the marble observatories of Samarkand—all this, as well as the singing and music of the Middle East, has its roots in ancient Persia. It is also said that sherry, or *Jerez*, which we get from Spain, was originally an imitation of the grape wine which in the Middle Ages was produced in Shiraz in southern Persia . . .

A while after our arrival at the tea-house a man in a European suit and soft-brimmed hat entered. All conversation came to a standstill as he walked to the centre of the room, raised his arm, and began reciting poetry. He was one of the wandering story-tellers who are the bards of Persia.

I doubt whether there is a country where poetry is more appreciated than in Persia. In every town and village you find streets and squares named after Persian poets, only one of whom is well known in the West. Who hasn't heard of Omar Khayyam's hymns to love and wine—life is short, enjoy it while you can! The Persians do not consider Omar Khayyam one of their great poets. These are Saadi, Hafiz and Ferdowsi, and all Persians will occasionally embellish their speech with quotations from their works.

The most popular poems tell of the exploits of Persian kings since the days when Cyrus the Great founded the first dynasty. Armies clash in great battles, pyramids are built of severed heads and scimitars flash while the tea grows cold in the glasses. Every eye is on the storyteller who illustrates his tale with dramatic gestures. He gasps in fear, laughs contemptuously, stamps his foot triumphantly.

In between the battles we heard poems about wine, love and philosophy. Most of the great thinkers of Persia have delved into mysticism to find an explanation to the puzzle of life—perhaps unconsciously to escape from the grim realities. They show a tolerance of other religions which is surprising in a Mohammedan country.

> Whence the charm of a fair face?
> Not earthly beauty only
> Can so allure us with its loveliness,
> We see as in a cloudy mirror
> The faint reflex of the perfect face.

Thus wrote a Persian poet nearly seven hundred years ago. Another, the beloved Hafiz, who died in 1389, expresses respect for Christianity. (European bards would hardly have got away with defending Islam in those days.)

> Where the turbaned anchorite
> Chanteth Allah day and night,
> Church bells ring the call to prayer
> And the cross of Christ is there.

The faces of the listeners grow serious when the storyteller recites such verses. They nod thoughtfully and take a sip of tea. It is hard to tell whether it is merely the rhythm of the verses that appeals to them.

Abdul and I had caused quite a stir when we entered,

but when we left again, full of tea, nobody took notice. The storyteller had started describing a new war, another battle . . .

Shortly before seven we returned to the rug factory. It was dark now; the only light came from two electric bulbs high up under the ceiling, so the children had to sit with their noses close to the carpets. In the morning they had chatted occasionally, but now they were silent. Their tired, serious faces and drooping shoulders made them look like old people.

The director came over and said that Ishia's parents had turned down my request. I asked Abdul to inquire why, but he begged to be excused. "Such a question would reveal boundless ignorance on your part," he explained. Obviously it was because she was a girl.

"But she's only seven!" I exclaimed.

That made no difference. Her reputation would be ruined just the same, and it would be impossible to get a decent bride price for her.

I pointed at the nearest boy, a little fellow with a woollen cap on his close-cropped head. Could I go to his home instead? The boy's father, a thin, bent man who was working next to him, hesitated a moment before he nodded.

While they finished working we talked to the director. He told us that the price of Persian rugs had been pressed further and further down during the last few years by machine-made goods. The costs were so high that it hardly paid to produce hand-woven rugs any more. More than a third of the rug factories in town had closed down already and he was afraid he would have to do so too.

When he received an order for a rug he would go to a

11. A village in southern Persia. The rounded roofs are built of clay – thus making roof beams unnecessary, wood being expensive in this part of the country.

12. Unemployment is ever-present in Persia, especially in the south where this picture was taken. Many are peasants, out of work because of the drought which has now lasted five years.

13. When the peasants have formed a co-operative society, each family can borrow 300 tomans from the government. The majority are unable to write their names, so they simply sign the receipt with a fingerprint.

14. A camel caravan passes through an oasis in Persia's vast southern desert.

foreman—they were the ones who called out the colours. Each foreman had five or six workers under him. They would agree on a price for the rug, and the director would supply the tools and raw materials. He also had to give the foreman a couple of thousand tomans in advance.

Sometimes a foreman would disappear with the money. You also risked getting a rug that only contained half as many knots as specified in the agreement—this meant less work, and therefore lowered the value of the rug. There wasn't much one could do in such a case.

He might also lose money when it came to selling rugs. The buyers, who exported them to Europe, did not have to pay until after three months. Sometimes they were late, and sometimes they didn't pay at all . . .

A moment ago I had considered the director a heartless exploiter. Now I thought of him as a nice and friendly man caught in circumstances beyond his control and worried about the future.

At seven o'clock we went off with the stoop-shouldered man who held his son by the hand. The boy, whose name was Golam, was nine years old. The distance between the street lamps became further and further apart as we walked. Finally, when there were none at all, we reached a cluster of earthen huts which looked extremely dilapidated even in the dark.

"This is where we live," Golam's father had stopped in front of a faintly illuminated door. With a dignified gesture he asked us to enter the tiny room which was his home. His wife, who was pumping a primus, quickly drew her *chadur* over her face. In the light of a flickering lamp I saw that a child lay sleeping on the clay floor. In a niche stood a wooden chest with some bedding on top of it. On the wall hung some clothes, a couple of family photographs and the inevitable picture of the Shah.

"Unfortunately I cannot offer you tea," Golam's father said, spreading a worn carpet on the floor for me to sit on. Perhaps that was why he hesitated before he agreed to let us come. For Persians it is shaming not to be able to bid a guest welcome with a glass of tea. He and Golam sat down opposite us. They were ready to answer questions.

I did not take out my notebook. People become self-conscious when you write down what they say. If you want them to speak freely, you have to give them your full attention.

Golam's father had been a carpet weaver all his life. He had learned the craft from his father and was now teaching it to his eldest son. The two boys were all they had left of ten children, the others having died in infancy. Golam had begun to work two years ago. He made one toman—slightly less than a shilling—a day. His father made five.

Last year they had sent Golam to school. He wanted so much to study, but unfortunately it had not worked out.

"Why not? Did he find it too difficult?"

"No, not at all—in fact he was one of the best in his class," his father replied with pride. Golam had stopped for quite a different reason. Prices had gone up and up during the last few years, but not the wages of rug weavers, and they had not been able to manage without the extra toman which the boy earned. The father had tried to earn more by working on Fridays, the Mohammedan Sunday, but he became ill from overwork and had to give it up.

Golam, who had intelligent brown eyes, listened intently

to everything we said. His face showed no sorrow when his father explained why he had to leave school. It was fate, there was nothing one could do about it.

Six months ago Golam's little brother, who was five years old, had also started working at the factory. He earned only half a toman, but the extra money had permitted them the luxury of tea and sugar every day.

Things had worked out fairly well until a month ago. Then calamity struck the little family. The younger boy had fallen from a scaffold at the rug factory and broken his leg.

The father raised the rug from the sleeping boy so we could see that one leg was in a cast. The boy had to go to the hospital—a government hospital which was supposed to treat the poor free of charge; but in fact you had to give something to be admitted. A present in the form of cash also helped the doctor to find time to operate.

The rug weavers were not covered by any kind of insurance. Golam's father had been forced to borrow fifty tomans from the director, and they had come to owe the grocer nearly the same amount. When you had already tightened your belt to the last notch, it was not easy to be rid of such a debt, especially because he had to pay the director five tomans a month in interest.

How much? Five tomans, he repeated, as if puzzled by my surprise. That was what one usually paid for a loan if one did not own any property or had no guarantor.

He was not complaining because of the low wages or the long working day, only because of the stroke of bad luck. If they could only recover from that they would be all right again, and give thanks to God . . .

All I had on me was fourteen tomans. This I gave him,

and then hurried away to escape their thanks. On the way home I asked Abdul if he thought me a soft touch. "No!" he exclaimed, and knowing that he had no illusions about the goodness of his fellow beings I believed him.

"There is no need to invent stories like that here in Iran," he continued with unexpected heat. "Almost everybody has problems like that, and many are much worse off. Iran is a rotten country, a hopeless country."

In the darkness I could hear him draw a deep breath. It sounded like a sigh of relief that now it had been said. Then he added in his usual tone of voice: "But there's nothing one can do about it. It is fate."

CHAPTER TEN

PERSEPOLIS

OUR BUS REACHED Persepolis just before dusk. Long shadows from the mountains moved slowly across the wide plateau where the kings of Persia had their capital until their power was broken by Alexander the Great. In the hazy light it was somehow easier to imagine how the city had looked that day more than two millenniums ago, when the young conqueror made his entry.

He came from the north, after having crushed the Persians in a decisive battle in the neighbourhood of Ekbatana, as Hamadan was called in those days. The victorious army advanced along the paved road which, in ancient times, ran all the way from the Mediterranean to Persepolis and on to the Persian Gulf. The Greeks must have looked in wonder at the great stone gate which gradually raised its head above the open plain. It was almost like the gateways leading to their own cities—but it stood there all by itself. The capital of the Persian empire was not even protected by a wall!

The ancient Persians were horsemen. They were used to moving about with their cattle and could not comprehend the mentality which made the Greeks cluster together behind walls. Or perhaps they understood that if an enemy came so far, everything was lost anyway.

A few hundred yards from the ruins of this gate the road makes a turn, and suddenly Persepolis emerges at the foot of a great rock, bathed in the last rays of the setting sun. Broad stone steps lead up to an immense platform where gigantic stone blocks lie scattered. Here and there stand remnants of the walls on which the Persian kings wrote the stories of their exploits in reliefs.

In endless rows the bearers of tribute come from the lands ruled by the Persians. There are bearded Assyrians, effeminate Egyptians, Babylonians with naked torsos and long-nosed Georgians, all weighed down with gifts.

From clay tablets found in the ruins we know what the vassal kings paid to Persepolis in tribute. The Babylonians sent five hundred eunuchs a year, the Medians one hundred thousand sheep, from Armenia came thirty thousand horses, from the Caspian Sea area one hundred virgins and one hundred young men, Arabia shipped incense . . . on and on goes the list, and every one had to bring gold on top of that.

Stone columns in rows point silently towards the sky, long since released from the weight of the spacious roofs that once covered them. Here lay the throne hall whose luxurious ornamentation has an Egyptian flavour. You also still find ruins here of heavy-looking buildings which bring Babylonian architecture to mind. The powerful figures of bulls which stand close by speak of Assyrian influence. And thus was the realm of the Persians a combination of all that was best from the conquered territories, fused into a new and unique culture.

In the side of a nearby rock has been hewn a horseman on his steed. It is a Persian king, wearing a coat of mail and wide trousers almost exactly like those used by some of the nomads today. The horse is also protected by a coat of mail, and behind it comes the heavily-armed retinue . . .

The figures bring to mind the knights of Europe, and some historians are convinced that the spirit as well as the arms and costumes of the age of chivalry came into being in Persia more than a thousand years before they reached us. By then, they had long since been forgotten in their homeland.

The faces of the horsemen have all been chipped off. " The blasted Arabs! " I muttered, for it was they who had done this wanton destruction when they conquered Persia in the seventh century. In their fear that man should worship idols they defaced all human figures they came across. " Barbarians! " I added darkly.

" Once in Mexico you said exactly the same thing," Chi-yun remarked. " You were furious because the Spanish monks had burned all the native documents."

I winced. Yes, we Europeans were no better—hundreds of years after the Arab invasion of Persia, we forced our religion on the people of the New World with fire and the sword . . .

The terrace with its temples and palaces was only the nucleus of the city which Alexander took without resistance. On the plain surrounding it, few signs of habitation have been found, so the population must have lived in tents. On the ancient Persian rock carvings are depicted tents very much like those used by the nomads today.

Alexander pitched camp some distance from the city. It

is likely that he really intended to spare Persepolis, for he was a great admirer of Persian culture. Both his wives were Persian, and he let six hundred of his officers take Persian princesses as wives, and ten thousand of his soldiers marry Persian women.

But on reaching the royal palace Alexander's troops saw a group of their countrymen who had been taken prisoners by the Persians. Several of them were horribly mutilated. This could have happened on the battlefield, but the Greeks believed that the Persians had tortured them after they had been taken prisoner. This infuriated them so much that they looted the city and put it to the torch.

Persepolis must have contained immense riches. Greek historians tell us that three thousand camels and ten thousand donkeys were requisitioned to carry away the contents of the Persian treasury and supply depots.

The temples and palaces burned for weeks. When the excavations were first begun late in the last century, the ruins were covered by a layer of ashes thirty inches deep. What was found under the ashes became an important part of the mosaic of ancient Persian culture which scientists have been able to piece together out of countless fragments.

The picture differs widely from the one we learned at school. We were taught to see the Persian kings as barbaric despots who attacked the democratic, freedom-loving Greeks. This may be partly because all the information we have of the Persians has reached us from the Greeks who feared and hated them.

In fact, the Persians were in many respects much more humane and tolerant than the Greeks. Greek society in those days was based on slavery. The ancient Persians did not exploit human beings in this way. On the contrary, in every place they conquered, one of their first acts was to free the slaves.

Under the first Persian kings there was complete religious freedom. Theirs was the first world empire where peoples of many races and creeds could live peacefully together. *Pax Persica* was the forerunner of *Pax Romana,* and one finds many Persian traits in the state which the Romans were to build later. The Roman empire had the same division into provinces, each headed by a governor. There was the same net of strategic roads, all leading to Persepolis. And the Persians minted the first coin which was valid everywhere within the borders of a great empire.

In Athens, Socrates had to drink the hemlock juice because he instilled dangerous thoughts in the minds of young men. It speaks for the tolerance of the Persian rulers that several Greek thinkers, among them Themistocles, sought refuge at the Persian court to escape the persecution of their zealous countrymen.

The Greek historian, Xenophon, who visited Persia about a century after the foundation of the empire, expresses admiration for the Persians. " In every Persian city there is a square where trading is prohibited and where the young are taught in different age groups," he wrote. Education was mainly in the form of discussions of real or imaginary problems.

" The Persians send their children to school so that they may learn about justice the same way we send our children to school to learn the alphabet," Xenophon continues. " To break a promise they consider the greatest of all sins . . ." One can understand that this made an impression on him, for even then the Greeks had the reputation of being the most cunning of all traders.

Judging by the scant historical information available, Cyrus, the founder of the empire, was by far the greatest of the Persian kings, both as a conqueror and as a human being. He was the son of a minor chieftain who was a vassal of the powerful king of Ekbatana. One cannot help wondering how Cyrus and his band of horsemen succeeded in reducing the heavily fortified city. It is known that the king of Ekbatana was a hated tyrant, and perhaps his subjects opened the gates for Cyrus, who had the reputation of being a just and honest man.

When Cyrus some years later advanced against Croesus of Lydia, the rich king sent a numerically superior army against him, probably composed of mercenaries. Again Cyrus was victorious, according to some reports because he had learned that the horses of the Lydians were not used to camels. When a herd of the gangling desert animals came charging against the Lydian cavalry, the horses panicked and stampeded.

His next goal was Babylon, in those days the largest city in the world. His coming had been foretold by the handwriting on the wall of King Nebuchadnezzar. Many believed that this Babylonian empire would prove too hard a nut even for the mighty Persians to crack. A frontal attack against the great walls would indeed have been suicidal, but one night the Persians diverted the waters of the river that flowed under the city into an empty reservoir. While Babylon slept, the Persians crawled in through the sewers and overpowered the defenders.

The Persians did not celebrate their victories with the

blood-baths usual in those days. When Cyrus had taken a city he released all slaves and prisoners of war and proclaimed that as long as the people obeyed the law he would leave them alone. Minor kings were permitted to remain in power if they recognized his suzerainty.

He gave the Jews of Babylon a present of money so that they could return to their homes and rebuild their demolished temple. Many chose to remain, so they must have felt secure under the Persians.

When Cyrus was killed in a skirmish with a wild nomadic tribe in what is now Afghanistan, his successors continued to expand the empire. The Greek city states in Asia Minor, which had been ever warring against each other, finally found peace under the Persians. Egypt fell; and here Persian engineers built a canal from the Nile to the Red Sea. The Armenians and the Georgians also came under Persian protection.

One day Xerxes knocked at the gates of the Greek motherland, but here the " barbarians " were finally stopped. To the Persians, this was probably only a distant border skirmish.

When Alexander came in 330 B.C., the Persian realm was greater than ever, but the Persians had lost their strength. Decadence, which is the fate of every conqueror, had already set in. One cannot live in luxury without turning soft.

With Alexander's victory at Ekbatana, the Persian kingdom collapsed. For a couple of hundred years it was divided between Hellenistic regents who retained power after the death of Alexander. Then it came under Persian rule again, and—with the exception of two barbarian invasions—remained so until the Arab conquest in 654 A.D.

One of the stone reliefs which has been found in the ruins of Persepolis shows King Darius on his throne. His eyes gaze at the plateau from which he once ruled over most of the then known world.

" I am Darius, the great King, the King of Kings," the inscription reads. " I rule over many peoples and many lands. Oh man, this is Ahuramazda's command to you; think no evil, do no evil . . ."

One cannot help admiring a god which not only preaches justice and tolerance, but also succeeds in making his followers live by them. This Ahuramazda must be worth learning more about, I thought, and to do so became my next goal.

CHAPTER ELEVEN

THE ETERNAL FLAME

INSTEAD OF THE expected servant, a middle-aged man in dressing-gown and slippers opened the door. He had deep-set grey eyes, a broad forehead and a prominent nose. After having made certain that he understood English I told him who I was.

"I would like very much to learn something about your religion," I concluded. This was a strange request from a stranger you have just set your eyes on, but Mr Jamshid welcomed me as if we were old friends and asked me inside.

The room was furnished in European style, but without the tawdriness one finds in most middle-class homes. His pretty, dark-eyed wife came forward to meet me without a veil. It was pleasant for once to be able to see the face of the woman who greeted me.

In Persia it is customary for the wife to leave the room as soon as she has served tea to the male guests, but Mrs Jamshid stayed with us. Her open and friendly manners made it obvious that she did not feel in the least like the Mohammedan women who are denied admittance to the men's world. Like her husband, she spoke English fluently

—they were both university educated—and several times during the conversation she stated her opinion.

"Have you seen the fire temple?" Mr Jamshid began. This is the main attraction in Kerman, an oasis town in south-eastern Persia which I was visiting. Here live some five thousand people who still worship the god of the ancient Persians, Ahuramazda. I nodded.

"And what do you think of our church?" he continued.

"I liked the smell of incense in the dark hall where white-robed priests kept the perpetual flame burning," I replied. "Unfortunately I could not understand a word of the prayers which they recited."

"Neither can I," Mr Jamshid put in. He explained that *Avesta,* the holy book of the ancient Persians, is written in a language which died out long before the birth of Christ. The present-day fire-worshippers learn their prayers from this book. "We know them by heart, but we don't understand a word," he added, shaking his head. "Even so we recite them by rote several times a day. It is really completely senseless."

At the fire temple I had been told that Mr Jamshid could tell me more than anyone else about Ahuramazda. This had made me assume that he was a deeply religious man, but his last remark seemed to indicate the opposite.

"But you find that in all religions," he continued. "Rituals are unavoidable, and they invariably lead to routine. What you saw at the fire temple was nothing but the shell of our religion."

"I was under the impression that you were—what shall I call it—a believer," I remarked. The word sounded strangely out of place in connection with a so-called heathen religion.

"And so I am," Mr Jamshid replied.

"Then you mean to say that you daily perform religious ceremonies which you consider meaningless?" I asked, almost indignantly, for it sounded as if the man was a hypocrite.

"Yes, of course," Mr Jamshid smiled. "What does it matter? Most people never really get to understand the higher meaning of a religion. For their sake it is necessary to maintain the outer forms of worship, for it is dangerous for man to live without religion."

"Why?" I asked. "In the West there are many who don't believe in God any more."

"Yes, and that is the underlying cause of most of your troubles," Mr Jamshid said. "The West is trying to replace God with science, with political idols like fascism and communism. But it doesn't work—at least, not in the long run."

He began to tell me about the founder of his religion, Zarathustra. Of course there were also many legends about his miraculous birth and life.

"This seems unavoidable in connection with the founders of the great religions. We really know very little about him except that he was a religious reformer like Mohammed, Buddha and the other great prophets. He rebelled against the worshipping of many gods. There was only one god, he maintained, and that was Ahuramazda."

Though he was persecuted by the priests, Zarathustra must have won many disciples. Shortly after his death, his teachings were made the state religion of Persia.

I nodded. "Yes, I have read about this. Do you think that religion had anything to do with making the ancient Persians so relatively humane and tolerant?"

"There was probably some connection," Mr Jamshid said. "Tolerance, moderation and honesty were the virtues especially advocated by Zarathustra—and compassion. We just cannot understand the god of the Jews and the Christians, who condemns the wretched sinner to eternal suffering in hell. We also have a hell in our religion, but it is only a place for a temporary sojourn."

He stopped and asked if I felt like a drink. I nodded gratefully. The great majority of Persians are Mohammedans, and in their homes not a drop is served. His wife poured us each a glass of the best home-made firewater I had ever tasted.

"Zarathustra probably lived about a thousand years before Christ," Mr Jamshid continued. "Many of his ideas continued to live in other religions. It is undoubtedly from us that the Jews got their belief in the resurrection of the body and eternal life—a belief which has later become part of Christianity as well as Mohammedanism. The Jewish belief in Satan and in reward or punishment in a future life also comes from our religion."

"What makes you think so?" I asked.

"Before the Jews were taken away as captives by Nebuchadnezzar these concepts did not exist in their sacred writings. They only appear after the return from Babylon, where the Jews can hardly have avoided contact with Persian fire-worshippers."

"What is the central idea in your religion, apart from the belief in a single God and the practice of tolerance?"

"What especially attracts me in the teachings of Zarathustra is that he always appeals to reason. Time and again he told his adherents to use their common sense. We must not accept something just because it appeals to us emotionally."

I expressed surprise that it had been possible for Zarathustra to found a religion on such premises.

"He probably did not consider himself the founder of a new religion," Mr Jamshid replied. "In fact, I doubt whether any of the great prophets did—excepting Mohammed. More likely, their followers later tried to put system into their preachings. I think it was in this way that religions became infused with miracles."

"What was it Zarathustra wanted people to accept with their reason?"

"He tried to explain to his fellow beings that there is an eternal struggle going on between good and evil. God created the earth so that man could assist him in his eternal fight with Ahriman, the ruler of the forces of evil. Here on earth, God can tempt evil into the open and then combat it through us, his representatives."

"It does not seem to me that we always behave like the representatives of God," I remarked.

"No, but that is because the struggle is also going on inside us. Every one of us has a free will. We know very well what is right and what is wrong. Every time we choose the right way, we have won a battle for God."

The name of the god of the fire-worshippers is composed of two words, Mr Jamshid explained. "*Ahura* means to be, to exist. Zarathustra wanted to show that existence is not only brute force, there is order and reason behind everything, so he added the word *mazda*, meaning spirit. Together they make up the omniscient intelligence, the absolute reality."

After a pause Mr Jamshid continued: "Zarathustra tried to explain that we should not create God in our own image, but that was of course too much to ask for. People have done just that from long before the dawn of history, and it is indeed difficult to visualize God as a concept, a law of nature. Ahuramazda shows himself in the fulfilment of this law—not by breaking it with miracles."

"You said it is from the fire-worshippers we got our belief in a life after death?"

"Yes, we do not believe that death puts an end to individual existence. There is no final extinction in nature. Nothing can disappear. In one way or another we continue in another form. What this form is, no human being can know—but those who have organized the different churches have without exception been tempted into acting as if they did know.

"For the fire-worshippers, the flame is the symbol of the change that is forever taking place in nature," he continued. "That is why there is always a flame burning in our temples—it represents everlasting life through perpetual change."

"You have talked about the struggle between good and evil. How do the fire-worshippers expect this struggle to end?"

"Of course there is no end to it, but few can grasp this, so Zarathustra told his followers that good would be victorious in the end. Possibly the priests added this after his death."

The fire-worshippers believe that *all* human beings—not just those who worship the right God—will dwell happily in paradise for ever once the forces of good have won the final victory. " What they are going to do there, our religion tells us nothing about," Mr Jamshid added with a gleam in his eye. " One wonders if it might not become monotonous."

He said that even before Alexander the Great conquered Persepolis, Zarathustra's message of man's freedom to choose between good and evil had all but disappeared within a hard shell of dogmas. The religion petrified into ceremonies that often had little meaning.

" The way we keep repeating prayers which we don't understand, for instance," Mr Jamshid continued. " And also our old custom of placing our dead in open towers. The priests must have misunderstood Zarathustra when he spoke of the fire as a symbol of eternal life. They thought he meant that fire was sacred, and must not be defiled by dead bodies. The same goes for the earth, which the priests also declared to be sacred, so the only way out was to let the birds consume the dead."

Most of the laws in his religion were fairly sensible, however. Thus polygamy and idleness were forbidden. It was considered wrong to live in celibacy, all people being in duty bound to reproduce themselves so that Ahuramazda will have many allies in his struggle against evil. But here, as in everything else, one ought to show moderation.

" You don't find families with a great number of children among us," Mr Jamshid said. The fire-worshippers are encouraged to drink wine, but to get drunk is considered a great shame. "Then the emotions get the upper hand," Mr Jamshid explained, "and Ahuramazda cannot make use of us. You have to keep your senses clear in the struggle against Ahriman, who is for ever striving to bring us out of balance."

Throughout the world there are about one hundred and fifty thousand fire-worshippers, of whom slightly less than half live in Persia, the remainder mainly in India. The latter are the *Parsees*, whose ancestors fled from Persia when the Arabs tried to force them to embrace Islam. Despite bloody persecution, a small group of faithful adherents continued to worship Ahuramazda secretly in the homeland of the ancient religion. The sacred fire was kept burning in underground temples of which a couple still exist.

Today you find fire-worshippers in most Persian towns, especially in the eastern part of the country. Though they make up only a tiny percentage of the population they exert great influence. Nearly ninety per cent of them have gone to school, compared to barely twenty per cent among the Mohammedans. Many are lawyers, doctors and engineers. There are also quite a few landowners; thus a whole district in the capital—*Teheran Pars*, it is called—belongs to the fire-worshippers, who undoubtedly constitute the most respected group in the country.

"You can trust them," I have heard several Persians say—a praise they seldom use in describing their countrymen.

Mr and Mrs Jamshid invited me for dinner, and afterwards we talked till far into the night. Before leaving, I asked my host why his faith had never become a world religion.

"That you must figure out for yourself," he replied with a smile. Did he mean that it is based too much on common sense? I am still wondering.

CHAPTER TWELVE

THE THIRSTY LAND

THE VILLAGE LAY at the end of a dusty lane winding through a field. It was surrounded by a wall, and where the wall had collapsed, round roofs could be seen like rows of beehives. Timber is expensive in treeless southern Persia, and to save on joists, the farmers build cupola-shaped roofs of clay.

" The place looks deserted," I remarked. The fields were not tilled and there wasn't a soul to be seen.

" It could very well be," replied Mr Wahdet, an English-speaking lawyer who had promised to show us how the farmers lived here. " Many have given up farming these days."

He slowed down, drove through the open gate leading into the village and stopped. A cock protested indignantly at the disturbance and strutted away at the head of his anxious harem. Some ragged children yelled with excitement and the women quickly pulled the *chadurs* over their faces. The men, who had been chatting in the shade of a tree, rose expectantly. The arrival of a jeep seemed to be quite an event in the village.

We sat down with the men and Mr Wahdet explained who we were. "I have told them you are English," he explained to Chi-yun and myself. "That is the only Western country they know."

The men watched us out of the corners of their eyes, their tight felt caps pushed to the back of their heads. If they found my Chinese wife un-English in appearance, their unshaven faces did not reveal it. They looked as if they were all related—each one had the same sharp nose and close-set eyes.

"Why aren't they working today?" I asked. All the men began talking. Mr Wahdet raised his hand. One at a time!

A skinny old man with deep lines around his mouth spoke first. You could not cultivate the fields without water, he said impatiently, as if it was something everybody should know. Oh, so there hadn't been enough rain this year? They shook their heads. They never got enough rain. But it wasn't that at all . . .

It took us nearly two hours to get the story pieced together. From time immemorial the people of this village had been tenant farmers, each family cultivating about ten acres. Formerly, the owner of the land had received four-fifths of the harvest.

"Four-fifths," I exclaimed. "What a blood-sucker!"

"No, that is not unreasonable," Mr Wahdet remarked. He explained that from ancient times it had been customary to divide the harvest into five equal shares. One share goes to the owner of the land, one to the supplier of water, one to the owner of plough and tools, one to the supplier of seed grain, and one to the man who does the work.

"In many places the farmers get three-fifths of the harvest," he added. "Then the landlord supplies only the land and the water."

One of the villagers had a radio, and a couple of years ago they had heard the Minister of Agriculture say in a broadcast from Teheran that a new day was beginning for the farmers of Persia. The government had decided to give them the land which they tilled.

In many villages the farmers had taken the law in their own hands and chased away the landlords. This had happened here, but when a commission from the Ministry of Agriculture came soon after to portion out the land, the farmers learned that they had to pay compensation to the landlord.

The compensation was cunningly calculated on a basis of how much the landowner had paid in taxes over the last ten years. Fortunately the local landowner had been an accomplished cheater, so they got the land at a bargain and were to pay over a period of fifteen years. The first installment was not due until the following year, so they had no immediate worry on that score.

Close to one-fifth of all cultivated land in Persia had already been affected by the land reform, Mr Wahdet said. In the hope that the programme they have started will somehow continue by its own momentum, the authorities have advised all landlords who have not yet been affected by the reform to part voluntarily with the major portion of their land. They can either rent the land out to the tenants on a thirty-year contract or sell it at a reasonable price. If they refuse to do either, the Ministry of Agriculture will step in with conditions which are considerably worse for the landlord.

It had of course been a joyful day for the farmers when the Shah arrived by plane and handed them their deeds in front of a whirring television camera. Complications had soon arisen, however. They had no oxen to plough with. The draught animals belonged to the landlord and he had taken them with him. If you wanted to rent oxen you had to pay cash. The farmers also had to have seed grain, but they had no money.

Around this time, a young employee of the Ministry of Agriculture had come to the village to advise the farmers. The government was going to help them, he said. If they would only start a co-operative, they could borrow money from the Bank of Agriculture.

They had never heard the word co-operative before, but it turned out to be quite easy to start one. They just had to pay half a toman each and elect a committee which again elected a chairman. When the farmers had done this, the young man from the ministry wrote to his superior that he had organized yet another co-operative.

" It can't be much of a co-operative," I remarked. " That sort of thing takes time. Even in my country where the farmers can read and write it took years to organize the co-operative movement."

" I know," Mr Wahdet replied. " Our co-operatives here in Persia are really nothing but credit organizations. But you have to start somewhere."

For several months after the founding of the co-operatives the farmers did not hear a word from the government, yet they had to plough and sow their fields. When it could not be postponed any longer they had gone to private money-lenders.

"How much interest do they have to pay?" I inquired.

"Five per cent."

"That's extremely reasonable," I said, surprised. You heard so much about usurious money-lenders in Persia.

"Five per cent a *month*."

"No, that's impossible—it must be a year!"

He shook his head. "That is not an unusual rate of interest for a private loan in this country. The bank charges 12 per cent a year, but that is only for people who can put up full security."

Some time later the farmers had received happy news from the Ministry of Agriculture. Now that they had joined the new co-operative movement the government would lend them three hundred tomans each at only six per cent a year.

When they received the money they signed the receipt with a thumbprint, for none of them could write.

Three hundred tomans! Never before had they owned so much cash. They slaughtered sheep and feasted. The wife got the trinket which she had wanted for so long. They also had to buy some new clothes instead of the old rags . . .

"Didn't any of them use the money to pay the debt to the moneylender?" I asked. One of the men nodded. Yes, he had paid what he owed. Two more had paid part of the debt. The others had not given it a thought until the three hundred tomans were gone.

"You can hardly blame them," Mr Wahdet said. "It was probably the first time in their lives that they had an opportunity to splurge."

Soon after this a terrible rainstorm had ravaged the district. The underground canal which brought water from the distant mountains was filled with mud. Formerly it had been the duty of the landlord to maintain the canal, but now the farmers were responsible themselves. It was a dangerous task requiring specialists, and to get the canal cleaned would cost many thousand tomans. No one would lend them so much money.

Then what had they done? They spread out their hands as if to show their helplessness. Nothing. What could they do apart from sitting here and waiting while the grain died of thirst?

That year the harvest had been only one-sixth of what it usually was, and when it again became time to plough and sow they had not done so. What was the use? After all, they knew that in these dry parts it was impossible to farm without irrigation. Since then they had neither ploughed nor sown.

But what did they live on? In the sugar beet season some of the men worked at a nearby sugar factory, but that didn't last for more than a couple of months. Quite a number of the young people had gone to the cities to look for work, but there were so many unemployed already. Those who stayed behind had become used to drinking tea without sugar, and later, to slaking their thirst with hot water.

Matters became even worse when they had to pay the first instalment on the land as well as the interest on the three hundred toman loan from the Bank of Agriculture. The Ministry of Agriculture winked at it if you failed to pay, but the Bank of Agriculture insisted on getting its due, even if it had to be collected by the Shah's bailiff.

Many farmers had been forced to go to the private moneylenders again.

Then the land reform had not helped them at all, I exclaimed. They were even worse off than before!

They sat for a while and looked musingly ahead as if they could not really grasp the thought. Yes, it was true that they were worse off than before. On the other hand, the land reform was a good thing if the government would only help them. . .

"But the government has neither the trained men nor the capital to take over the functions of the landowners," Mr Wahdet put in. "That is why the farmers are suffering in many of the areas where land reform has been carried out."

"But what can the poor people do?" Chi-yun asked.

"There is one way out for them," Mr Wahdet replied. He explained that well-to-do city people were secretly buying the land which the farmers had taken over. This had happened in many places. The people involved would sign a kind of secret contract—*bunchag,* it was called—which one could be forced to honour even though the transaction was unlawful. The new landlord takes over the farmer's debts and rents the land to him under the same conditions as in the old days. Then the landlord is responsible for supplying plough, oxen and seed grain, and for maintaining the underground canals.

Actually, the government would have helped the farmers much more by investing in new wells and underground canals instead of by land reform, Mr Wahdet said. All over Persia there was plenty of idle land because of insufficient water. It would be much more useful for the country to bring new land under the plough than to parcel out the land already under cultivation.

" But of course the land distribution makes a much better impression," he concluded. " Politically, that is."

" Then the farmers have not really gained anything by the land reform?" I asked.

" They have, for when the *bunchag*-contract is signed, the farmer gets a small cash payment. Of course most of them blow the money, but then at least they have had the fun of doing it. And under the new contract, the farmer usually gets a slightly larger share of the harvest. Then the land no longer belongs to him, but at least it is preferable to the situation which these people are in now."

I looked at the ragged farmers, the skinny kids with stomachs that bulged with intestinal worms. The one bright spot in their future was a rumour that next year the government would grant each family a new loan of three hundred tomans. This would help a little, but it would not stop the vicious circle. It seemed that nothing could stop it . . .

Mr Wahdet was to appear in court that afternoon, so we had to leave. The farmers stood at the gate and watched us until we disappeared in a cloud of dust. It was not every day that a jeep came to the village.

CHAPTER THIRTEEN

THE ROAD TO BANDARABBAS

AT A PARTY in Teheran we met a Danish engineer who had spent nearly thirty years in Persia. When I remarked that he must have seen many interesting places on his journeys here, he shook his head. Apart from Isfahan and Persepolis, which of course were of historical interest, you found the same brown clay huts everywhere.

"What is the worst place you have been to?" I asked on a sudden impulse.

"Bandarabbas," he replied without hesitation. "That is the hottest and dirtiest of all the miserable towns in the whole Persian Gulf. You certainly wouldn't find anything to write about there."

Surely there was something to tell about a place which had made such a strong impression on him? Nothing that he could think of. The population was a dirty lot, composed of Arabs, Indians and negroes with a sprinkling of Persian criminals . . .

Criminals?

Yes, from way back the Persian authorities had deported unwanted elements to Bandarabbas. That was why many called it "The Persian Siberia". The women wore black masks instead of the *chadur,* no one knew why. It had always been one of the poorest areas in the country, and the situation was especially bad at present as not a drop of rain had fallen for several years . . .

"Is it possible to go there by bus?" I asked.

"I think so, but if you are thinking of making a trip to Bandarabbas I'd advise you to fly. The roads are unsafe in that part of the country and there's lots of malaria. My company has a man down there. Of course you can stay with him."

I put Bandarabbas on our travel route. You go there from Shiraz, a large oasis town in southern Persia. The day before we were supposed to leave, however, Chi-yun came down with dysentery. I felt quite sorry for myself when I kissed her goodbye before dawn one morning and wandered off to the bus station. When you are used to having a companion it is no fun to travel alone.

In the packed bus I luckily got a seat next to a young carpenter who spoke a little English. He worked at Kuwait, the fabulously wealthy sheikdom at the northern end of the Persian Gulf. Here, oil gushes out whenever you drill a hole in the ground, but there is a great scarcity of water, which is imported from Persia.

Like many other poor Persians he had moved to Kuwait, attracted by the high wages. He had been home to visit his family and was now going back to work.

It was still dark when we finally left. The bus hopped and skipped on the wretched road, but I soon heard snoring from my neighbours. Even those who were standing up managed to doze off once in a while.

In the middle of the desert the driver suddenly stepped

on the brakes. Some figures with guns were standing in the road, and in the faint light it was hard to tell whether they were bandits or soldiers.

"It's a military patrol," the carpenter said, relieved. An officer shouted something to the driver, a soldier jumped in, and we drove on, but now nobody slept. What had happened? Why did we have an escort?

There were bandits in the vicinity, the soldier replied. They had robbed a caravan and fired at motor-cars!

The "bandits" were probably just poor people who had lost their cattle in the drought, said the carpenter. Many of the nomads were starving, and it was impossible for them to find work.

"It isn't everybody who can go to Kuwait," he concluded, smiling happily at the thought of his own luck. We did not see any bandits, but the drought had left its mark. Farms and villages were deserted. The desert was reclaiming the land which man had wrested from it.

During the morning we saw only one inn which had not closed down. The subsoil water had fallen catastrophically due to the lack of rain, the owner told us. The wells dried out, and you could only get water by drilling far down with modern equipment. Few could afford that.

I couldn't get a bite down of the tough mutton and bread which was all we could get to eat. When we left we brought along a jar of water for some soldiers who had headquarters in the ruins of a fort. They were supposed to be fighting bandits, but did not seem to take their task too seriously. As soon as they had received the water they went back to their game of cards.

That afternoon we saw only two inhabited houses and a

15. There is something uncanny about the black masks which have a small pin sewn along their middle to keep the shape. The practice probably originates from Arabia.

16. More than two-thirds of Persia is desert and so the camel is still the most important form of transport.

camel caravan. The clumsy animals walked in a long row, swaying gently under their burden of human beings and bulging saddlebags. When the car approached, a man jumped down and ran towards the road. He shouted something, holding up an empty water bag, but we had no water to spare for the nomads.

On the top of a hill lay the ruins of a huge fire temple. For more than two thousand years the burned bricks had resisted the wear and tear of time. Once there must have been a large town at the foot of the temple, for you could see the remnants of great walls and the outlines of countless houses. The place was littered with broken potsherds, glazed in strong, pure colours.

Now there wasn't a soul living within miles, and even weeds could not grow in the stony earth. Had the Arabs or the Mongols laid the town waste, or had it been deserted due to a change in climate, perhaps connected with erosion? Nobody knows, but perhaps the archaeologists will be able one day to dispel the darkness which covers long periods of Persia's past.

In the evening we arrived at a small town where we were to spend the night. Here we were told that we could not continue at daybreak as planned. There were bandits in the area, and no vehicle was permitted to leave the town until the following afternoon. Then we were to move in a convoy, protected by an armoured car.

At the only hotel in town I caused a stir by demanding a room for myself. It was customary that a group should share one of the cell-like cubicles, but if the spoiled foreigner was willing to pay to sleep alone, it was of course his own business.

Again, tough mutton and bread were the only fare, but now it tasted delicious, especially with beer, which I could fortunately get. I tried hard to drown my sorrow at being delayed in this God-forsaken place, but without success. Fuming with indignation, I finally asked the carpenter why we could not get off until the afternoon of the following day. Who had decided that, anyway?

"Does it matter?" he replied with a yawn. "We couldn't do anything about it, anyway, so why worry?"

Such an outlook comes naturally to an Oriental who has learned to bow to his fate, but I declared that I would be damned if I would sit here and do nothing all next day! As soon as it got light I would go out on the main road. There might be a car going to Bandarabbas despite the order to drive in convoy.

"But what would be the use?" my friend asked. "The bus company won't give you back your money, so you would have to pay twice for the stretch from here to Bandarrabas."

"So what? After all, that would only be a matter of a few tomans—eight or ten, at the most."

"You mean that you would pay ten tomans to get off some hours earlier?" he inquired. When I nodded he looked at me wonderingly.

"Why are you Europeans always in such a hurry?" he asked. Before I fell asleep I lay for a while thinking of his words. Yes, why are we in such a hurry?

Dawn found me on the road, and there I remained while the sun crept slowly across the sky. I was at the point of giving up, when an old station wagon came rattling along in a cloud of dust. I waved it to a stop.

"Bandarabbas?" I shouted, and the driver nodded. That was about the extent of my Persian, so I pointed at myself and spread out my hands. That was my way of asking whether they had room for me, but I immediately realized that the question was superfluous. A station wagon can take eight at a pinch, but there were already ten people jammed inside, and lots of luggage.

The driver nodded again and held up nine fingers to show how many tomans I had to pay for the ride. When I had given him the money he miraculously succeeded in making room for me between himself and his young assistant. I couldn't actually get in contact with the seat, but the assistant handed me an oil tin on which I put a newspaper to save my pants. It was a bit hard to sit on, but far better than standing bent over.

The driver pointed to himself, said "Isfahan," and looked questioningly at me. Where was I from?

"Dan*mark*," I replied, with the emphasis on the last syllable the way it is pronounced in Persian, but no one in the car had ever heard of such a place.

"Inglis?" someone suggested. This means English, and I nodded, for that was probably as close as we would ever get to it. The next moment I gasped, for the driver had suddenly let go of the wheel with both hands to draw two telling curves in the air in front of him. He winked and again looked questioningly at me. Was I married?

When I nodded he held his hand a short distance from the floor. Any children? I nodded again. How many? his glance inquired. At the sight of my index finger he burst out laughing and held up five, then two fingers, and pointed at himself. That was how many kids he had!

After this conversation nothing was said for a long time. We squinted against the strong light from the desert which lay motionless under quivering waves of heat. What if something happened to the car? It was a chilling thought, for days might pass before the convoy came.

Late in the afternoon I was sure I saw a mirage, but the river which had suddenly appeared in the middle of the desert turned out to be real enough. A lot of rain must have fallen on some distant mountains. When we were out in the middle of the current, the engine suddenly spluttered and died out. Loudly the man began asking Allah to help us, and we needed it. The water came up to the engine, and the powerful current tugged at us, but fortunately the motor got started again and slowly pulled us to safety on the opposite bank. "Yah, Allah!" they shouted in a chorus and bowed their heads in gratitude. That the driver had changed to four-wheel drive seemed unimportant to them, or perhaps they had not even noticed it, so certain were they that it was Allah who had helped us.

For a moment I had a vague feeling of envy. It seemed a long time ago that we in the West had believed so fervently in anything.

Shortly after dark we saw many lights ahead of us. "Bandarabbas!" the driver said happily, but suddenly a flame leaped out from under the dashboard. The motor coughed a couple of times and then stopped.

We took turns striking matches while the driver and his assistant tried to find out what was wrong. It turned out that the main electrical wire had burned out, and we kept on burning matches while they worked to fix it with a piece of the wire leading to the rear light. They had only a monkeywrench and a screwdriver for tools, but began undaunted to bite and tear the wire apart, until I remembered my pocket knife and lent it to them.

When we had used up all the matches we made little torches of the newspaper I had been sitting on. The assistant was about to tear off a new sheet, when he suddenly gave a shout that sent the others running to his side. In silent admiration they stared at a picture of Brigitte Bardot in all her semi-naked splendour. They sighed when she too had to go up in flames. After that we took turns sucking energetically at a cigarette; the faint glow made it possible to see a little.

Finally they had finished, but the wire burned out again as soon as we started the engine. The driver raised his arms in despair, then pointed to the ground. We might as well lie down and sleep, for here even prayers were of no avail.

The other passengers began dragging their bedding out of the car, but I pointed at my legs and said " Bandarabbas." Even if I had to walk I would get there tonight!

They shook their heads and the assistant moved his hand across his throat to show what I risked if I walked along here at night, but my mind was set on food, a hot bath and a clean bed at the home of the Danish engineer in Bandarabbas. I took my suitcase in one hand, the bag with my photographic equipment in the other, and set off resolutely.

I had not gone far before the driver and his assistant came hurrying after me. They must have been exhausted and would undoubtedly have preferred to sleep, but thought it unsafe for me to go alone in the darkness.

I did know how to count in Persian, and could take part in a discussion about how many miles we had ahead of us. Our guesses ranged between two and three. I walked in front, wading through the ankle-deep dust with long, dogged steps, but after about an hour I began to lag behind even though the two others had long since taken my luggage. The lights seemed to be just as far away as ever.

Later I learned that we had covered nine miles by the time we finally reached town. When we asked for Kampsax, the Danish engineering firm, we were directed to a large building gleaming with lights. The door was opened by a servant who looked sceptically at the dirty figures outside. When I spoke to him in English he smiled and took me to the young engineer and his wife, who received me with open arms. Food and drinks were put on the table, and a hot bath was drawn for me.

I was about to mention my two companions, but suddenly I felt embarrassed. It seemed quite enough trouble for one man to show up in the middle of the night, I thought as I walked back to the front door.

My two friends were still standing there, looking wide-eyed at the wonders inside. The icebox, the comfortable furniture, the swimming pool in the background—it all belonged to a world which they did not know. When I explained that I was staying on they smiled, happy that I was going to live at such a nice place. I tried to give them some money, but they shook their heads. That wasn't why they had accompanied me, their reproachful looks seemed to say, but I did succeed in making the assistant accept my pocket-knife, which I had seen him admire.

Long after they had disappeared in the darkness I kept on

seeing their faces. I felt as if two good friends had gone out of my life, but the next day I was to meet them again —under quite unexpected circumstances.

CHAPTER FOURTEEN

THE BLACK MASKS

" YES, WE HAVE had *one* exciting experience since we came here," the wife of the young engineer said. We were lying next to the swimming pool, sipping orange juice. It was seven o'clock in the morning and the temperature was still bearable in Bandarabbas.

" What are you talking about?" asked her husband, Kurt.

" That time there was an epidemic of dysentery . . ."

" I don't know if you can call that an experience. After all, nothing really *happened,* and no one actually *accused* us of having eaten them."

" Eaten what?" I inquired.

" The children," he replied. " Yes, in a way it was quite exciting . . ."

During a violent dysentery epidemic in Bandarabbas some months ago, two children had disappeared. Simultaneously the workers who were building the new road for the Danish company had discovered that neither the Danish engineer nor his Armenian assistant had the disease. The connection was obvious to anyone who could add two and two together, for it was well known locally that eating the heart and liver of a child gave sure protection against sickness.

Until that time everyone had been kind to them—they were the only foreigners in town—but now they could sense a change. When they went for their usual evening walk, people shunned them. One day the Kampsax office was searched by detectives. Their car was stopped repeatedly by policemen who examined the luggage compartment. A guard was placed outside their door . . .

Here the engineer stopped. We could hear the purring of the air-conditioner.

"And what happened then?" I asked. "How did it end?"

"The epidemic stopped," he replied with a smile. "Then it was forgotten, people don't have a long memory here. It's too hot."

After breakfast and a last dip we went out in the hot sun, he to his road building, I to visit the market. I was accompanied by a young Kampsax employee who knew a little English. Fortunately we did not have far to go, for every time a truck came thundering by we nearly got lost in the clouds of dust it raised. Every now and then we would catch a glimpse of a city of sunbaked clay huts separated from the emerald-green water by a blinding white beach.

A long queue had gathered in front of a public standpipe. Water was precious here in town, the engineer had told me—two shillings and fourpence a cubic metre, to be exact. No wonder that only the two rich foreigners could afford a swimming pool.

The queue consisted mainly of women, and I am afraid that my sunglasses did not hide my open-mouthed staring.

The first time one sees the famous black masks one can hardly believe one's eyes. In Persia you don't find them anywhere outside Bandarabbas, and nobody knows why this macabre fashion took root here. There is something sinister about the faceless heads, with hollow eye-sockets. Beneath these death's heads are voluptuous figures in gaudy dresses and tight-fitting slacks . . .

It sounds enticing—until a little more local colour is added. Monkey-like babies clung to the ragged women whose unwashed bodies reeked of perspiration. Flies came buzzing from a nearby garbage dump to settle around the children's eyes and crawl under the masks of the mothers . . .

We could also hear a buzz from the market, where the voices of a great throng mingled with the cackling of chickens and the braying of donkeys. The market was held on the open beach. There were two parking places—one for camels, and one for the little boats of those who had come by sea. There were no motor-cars.

When I see a lot of good subjects for pictures, I go a little amuck, and that day it was especially bad. I dashed about among the traders, sticking my camera up in their faces. Half the time I forgot to measure the light, the other half I didn't focus properly. Of course one doesn't have time to see anything; all I remember is glimpses of colourful gowns, Persian faces with negroid noses, Indians with kinky hair, black Arabs. The sun shone on strange fishes drawn from the depths of the tropical ocean.

"How do you do?" asked an elderly man who sold poisonous-coloured plastic wares. He still remembered some of the English he had learned long ago in his home town, Isfahan. Why of all places had he settled down in Bandarabbas? Not for the fun of it, he replied. He had been exiled as punishment for a political crime of which, he assured me, he had been innocent. He was not the only one.

I would come and talk to him later, I said and hurried on to the next picture, but before I could snap it I felt a hand on my shoulder. A man in civilian clothes, very unshaven, showed me his police badge, pointed at my camera and shook his head vigorously. It was prohibited to take pictures.

If I had just nodded and smiled it would have shown my respect for authority and I could probably have continued my picture-taking in another part of the market. But I knew my rights—foreigners *are* in fact permitted to take pictures in Persia—and stuck by them. I even took a picture right in front of his nose. As a result he was forced to arrest me in order to save his face My interpreter whispered that a couple of tomans would straighten everything out, but I would not hear of that.

At the station it turned out that the question of whether I was permitted to take pictures did not interest the sergeant in charge at all. Together with a colleague who could read English he examined my passport and soon found my Persian visa. I had stayed in the country longer than I was supposed to, they declared triumphantly. My visa was issued in June and was only good for three months. We were now in October.

I explained that a visa is good from the day you enter the country, not from the date of issue, but they shook their heads. I had broken the law, and judging by their manner they were going to make me pay dearly for it.

Now something suddenly happened which made the

worm turn. "Eskelund, where are you?" a voice called in Danish. It was the wife of the Danish engineer who had gone to the market to fetch me, and through her servant had learned that I had been arrested. When I explained what had happened she turned to the sergeant and informed him politely that her husband was a good friend of the governor.

It is not nice to be vindictive, but I must admit that I enjoyed tremendously seeing the sergeant put on an ingratiating smile and admit that even he could have made a mistake. Wouldn't the lady please sit down? He sent for tea.

Now two men were led in. They had a policeman on either side and walked with their heads bent as one should when confronting persons of authority. I jumped up. It was my two friends from the night before—the driver and his assistant!

They were delighted to see me, for they were in a bad fix and thought that I as a foreigner could perhaps help them. After we had parted the previous evening they had walked back to the car with a piece of wire which they had bought in a garage. At dawn they had been arrested by a police patrol which had raised vague charges against them for vagrancy and the possession of a vehicle in improper condition. The latter accusation was especially unjust as virtually no vehicles in Persia are ever in a proper condition. Here the policemen had demanded fifty tomans and, when the driver refused to pay, had placed him and his assistant under arrest.

I don't know whether it was the invisible presence of the governor through my hostess that induced the sergeant to let my two friends off with a warning, but it is not improbable. I hope so, for I felt indebted to both of them. When we parted they gave me the big Persian embrace, with kisses on both cheeks.

The sergeant merely shook my hand and said he wished I would take many good photos in Persia. I intended to go back to the market and talk to the plastic seller, but nothing came of that. The engineer's wife invited me for a glass of beer, and when we got home there was a telegram for me from Chi-yun. I was to hurry back to Teheran. The Shah had promised us an interview on the forthcoming Saturday.

CHAPTER FIFTEEN

THE PEACOCK THRONE

WE HAD NEVER interviewed a Shah before. How were we going to address him? There were so many possibilities.

" King of Kings ", the first of Mohammed Reza Shah's impressive titles, sounded a bit high-flown. " Shadow of the Almighty " didn't have have quite the right ring in our democratic age either, nor did " Centre of the Universe . . ."

" I think we should just say ' Your Majesty '," Chi-yun broke into my monologue. We were sitting in the waiting-room of one of the Shah's five palaces in Teheran. Outside, palms raised their tufty heads over a well-kept park encircled by a tall iron fence. On the sidewalk in front of the fence, heavily-armed soldiers walked back and forth. The regular clicking of their heels mingled with the noises from the metropolis which raised its jagged profile in the background.

I rose and began pacing nervously up and down the largest and softest Persian rug I had ever set foot on. The polished mahogany furniture mirrored the sparkling crystal chandelier in the ceiling.

"No, 'Your Majesty' sounds too tame," I objected. "Then I prefer 'Occupant of the Peacock Throne' . . ."

Chi-yun's laughter was interrupted by the opening of a door. A tail-coated court attendant entered and asked us to follow him. We walked up a long, broad staircase and entered a dim library.

It seemed as if we already knew the tall, grey-haired man who came towards us, but then we had seen his picture in every Persian restaurant, institute and home we had been to. Usually he is in uniform, with one hand on the be-jewelled handle of his sword and row upon row of colourful medals on his chest. That is how the people expect their Shah to look.

Today he was wearing a dark suit and had a pair of reading glasses perched on his prominent nose. He greeted us in English in a friendly and informal way that at once put us at our ease. When he sat down opposite us, an almost inaudible sigh escaped him, and no wonder. We were number eight on his list of visitors for the day, and he had been Shah for twenty-two years.

I saw him glance suspiciously at the list of questions which I held in my hand. In his autobiography, *Mission for My Country,* he frankly states that supplying material to every wandering journalist can be a trying job. He speaks of "big, well-dressed, self-assured, impressive-looking American correspondents" who "seem more interested in the colour of my necktie than in my social convictions" and who have "with suave confidence written accounts composed of the most banal superficialities".

Reading this, I had promised myself not even to look at the Shah's necktie, but of course I couldn't help doing so now that I was sitting opposite him. It was dark blue.

At first we spoke of Persia's long history. The country lies on the ancient military route between east and west and has for thousands of years been exposed to foreign invasions. Alexander the Great was only one of many conquerors—just about all the barbarian nomads who came charging on their horses out of central Asia have at one time or another passed through Persia. By the time the Arabs, Mongols and Turks had invaded the country, little was left of the high moral standards of the ancient Persians.

Fate itself taught the Persians to look at life as a gamble beyond their control. " Drink today, and make love, for tomorrow may be the end ", was the advice of the great Persian philosophers. One understands why the most popular figures in Persian folk stories are the most cunning and ruthless. Survival was the most important thing, and those who came out on top in the struggle, were admired most, regardless of the methods they used.

The Shah did not mince his words when he talked about his own people. With an impatient frown he spoke of the tendency of some Persians " to lie whenever it suits them ". In his autobiography he mentions that during the Mongol invasion, lying was essential for survival.

" This point of view may serve as a historical explanation, but it is a poor excuse for those who lie today," he adds.

During these long periods of national upheavals, the giving and taking of bribes came to be looked on as something natural. Those in power did away with all possible competitors. Thus Shah Abbas, who is considered Persia's best ruler after the coming of Islam, had the eldest of his three sons strangled and the two others blinded. Then he felt a little less insecure.

What the Persians did not already know about cynicism, they learned from the Europeans when Russian and British interests clashed in the Middle East towards the end of the last century. The agents of the two great powers vied with each other to obtain concessions by bribery. Rights of exploitation were signed away in return for personal loans to the last rulers of the most corrupt dynasty in the long history of Persia.

When oil was found in the Persian Gulf, the hidden struggle for power nearly led to open war. To avoid this, the two giants signed an agreement making the northern part of the country a Russian sphere of interest, the southern a British. In between was a " neutral " zone where they both had a free hand.

The power of the dying Persian dynasty was further weakened when the nomadic tribes of the south went into the pay of the British, while the Russian trained a Persian Cossack regiment in their zone. When they could not get the Shah to toe the line in any other way, they would let these armed forces march on Teheran.

The Shah told us that as late as the thirties, London had officially warned Teheran not to send troops against the rebellious Bakhtiari tribes in the south as they were allies of Great Britain!

But during the ten years preceeding this incident, great changes had taken place in Persia. In the early twenties, the faltering Persian dynasty had been toppled by a dynamic officer who had risen from the ranks in the Persian Cossack regiment. This was Reza Shah . . .

The Shah involuntarily straightened himself when the name of his deceased father was mentioned. You could tell that he had great respect for him.

And not without reason. Reza Shah, who during his lifetime was hated by the intellectuals, is today spoken of with admiration by all Persians. In barely twenty years he brought Persia out of the Middle Ages. He united the country, put an end to foreign concessions, paid or cancelled the enormous national debt, built roads and railways. Only a ruthless man could accomplish all this, and he was ruthless. He loved his country and wanted more than anything else to give back the Persians their self-respect.

"Twice my father broke diplomatic relations with France because French journalists had written critically about Persia," the Shah told us with a smile, glancing significantly at me.

It made an unforgettable impression on the present Shah when, at the age of six, he saw his father mount the peacock throne. On the same occasion he was proclaimed Crown Prince. He had a strict upbringing—in his autobiography he tells how his father established the first modern military academy in Persia in order that his sons could go to a good school.

Later the young Crown Prince went to Switzerland and studied for four years. "I consider those years the most important in my whole life," he told us. "I learned what democracy is."

When he came home his father told him that he was going to marry an Egyptian princess. Reza Shah wanted a grandson. The constitution which had been granted in 1906—but never respected by anyone—required the wife of the Crown Prince to be of Persian origin. The old Shah got around this by ordering parliament to pass a law giving the princess Persian origin!

When the war broke out in 1939, Reza Shah was beginning to get the country whipped into shape. Like so many strong men in the under-developed world he was a great admirer of Hitler. This the Allies used as a pretext for occupying the country, for they had to have a supply line to Russia.

In the hope of thereby saving his dynasty, the proud old Shah abdicated in favour of his son.

When the young Shah spoke of this period, the wrinkles reappeared on his forehead. He had been in an impossible situation. With the Russians in the northern half of the country and the British in the southern he possessed no real power. How then could he retain the respect of the Persians by showing that he was as strong as his father?

Hardly had he ascended the throne before an attempt was made on his life. He was on his way to an inauguration ceremony, when a young man suddenly pulled out a gun and fired five shots at him at point-blank range. That he was hit by only two of them the Shah considers a proof that Providence holds a protective hand over him. One bullet hit him in the shoulder. The other went in through the cheek and came out under the eye. When I looked closely I could see a tiny scar.

After the war the Russians refused to withdraw their troops as promised. Two " People's democracies " were proclaimed in the northern zone under the protection of Russian bayonets. They were soon dissolved, however, when the Western powers warned Stalin that Persia lay within their sphere of interest.

The Russians withdrew, but left a dangerous virus behind in the form of the only effective political organization in the country. The "Tudeh", or "People's Party", as it was called, soon became extremely powerful, although it never got a majority in parliament. This may have been because the ignorant farmers were bribed to vote for the landlords.

A strange situation arose, with a conservative parliament whose actions were largely determined by the Tudeh-led mob in Teheran.

It was during this confused period that Mossadeq came to power. The old prime minister, who was fond of wearing pyjamas and had a fainting fit whenever things went against him, was respected by everyone for his honesty. He won great popularity by nationalizing the mighty Anglo-Iranian Oil Company which for years had existed as a state within a state. The Persians had to be satisfied with the crumbs which fell from the rich man's table. The state's income from oil has risen steadily since the nationalization of the company and today amounts to more than U.S. $200,000,000 a year.

But many thinking Persians consider the oil money a curse, since it has resulted in the neglect of other sources of income—especially agriculture. "It would be better for us if we had drilled for water instead of oil," I have heard several Persians say.

Under Mossadeq the nationalized oil industry came to a

standstill. Spoiled as it was by the oil income, the country had forgotten how to stand on its own feet and went bankrupt. Mossadeq finally lost control of the Tudeh-led masses which began looting in the capital. This was in the summer of 1953. The Shah fled to Rome.

How uncertain his position was is shown by a little story in his autobiography. The Shah kept a private car at the Persian embassy in Rome, but the *chargé d'affaires* was so convinced that the Shah would fall that he refused to give him the keys!

Two days later the Shah was called home. A general had pounded the table and said " enough of this nonsense." He sent tanks into the streets. When the mob heard the first shots they stopped toppling statues of the Shah and began instead to shout " Long live the Shah."

It is understandable if these occurrences convinced the Shah that Persia is not ripe for democracy in the Western pattern. From that day on he used a firm hand. First he crushed the Tudeh party. Then he dissolved the recalcitrant parliament which was still dominated by conservatives who refused to pass his land reform laws. After having ruled for three years without a parliament he appointed last winter a new legislative assembly, which was then duly elected by the people—there were no opposition candidates. Demonstrations against the government were put down ruthlessly with the loss of many lives.

" I still believe in democracy," the Shah said when we discussed his new " hard " line. " But not without discipline —then it is anarchy."

Today he sits more firmly in the saddle than at any other time since he became Shah. The intellectuals hate him, but he has an obedient parliament, an effective secret police and a loyal army. As everybody knows, he has greatly strengthened his position by finally, in his third marriage, producing an heir to the throne.

Towards the end of the interview he talked about the economic progress in his country. With sparkling eyes he described new dams, power stations, roads and railways. Now he was as enthusiastic as a boy talking about his toys.

As we listened I thought of the contrast between his optimism and the lack of spirit one sees everywhere in Persia. So many of the people we had met on our journey had dreamed of going to a foreign country—away from the hopeless poverty of Persia, from the tyranny of corrupt and inefficient officials. In the West there are tens of thousands of Persian students, many of them educated at the expense of the state, who do not want to return to their own country.

Corruption is still considered a natural thing in Persia, and everybody talks about the hundreds of millions which the Shah is suposed to have salted away in Swiss and American banks. People sound envious rather than indignant when they discuss this.

The Shah also spoke about his favourite project: the land reform. We told him that in some of the villages which we had visited, the farmers were so badly off that they were forced to sell secretly their newly-acquired land. In other villages they were becoming the tenants of wealthy city people.

The Shah listened politely. Yes, there had been a drought in many parts of the country, he said. The farmers suffered greatly in the stricken areas, but everything would be done to help them.

The drought had nothing to do with it, I said. The sufferings of the farmers were mainly caused by the lack of capital. Formerly, the landlords had supplied them with credit . . .

"Yes, and now the government does it through the co-operatives," the Shah interjected.

"But the farmers are badly off even in those places where co-operatives have ben organized," I continued. "The amount they can borrow from the state is quite insufficient, and they often use the money for useless things because they have no one to guide them."

The Shah made an impatient gesture with his hand. "The co-operatives will solve the problems," he said. "We have already organized three thousand of them. We will organize twelve thousand more within the next two or three years. It is the only way out . . ."

It sounded as if he was trying to convince himself. Now he looked much older than his forty-five years. I had a feeling that the weary old nation was speaking through him.

I thought of the farmers whose grain was withering because they did not have money for getting the underground canals cleaned, of the landless Kurdish nomads, the Turcomans who were worse off after they had become owners of land. They had all thought that everything would be all right if only the Shah heard of their problems, but now I understood how little he could do. Even if he had the best of intentions he could not single-handedly do away with the injustices and the dishonesty. His strong father tried to change the habits of the nation, but even he had not succeeded. Reza Shah forced Persia three steps forward, but as soon as the reins were slackened it took two steps backwards.

The Shah rose. The interview was over.

"There are many problems in this part of the world," he said as we shook hands. "But give me fifteen or twenty years and I'll make something out of my country. The most important thing is not to lose patience."

INDEX

Abdul, 21, 22-8, 32, 34, 41-2, 43, 50, 62, 63, 64, 68, 69, 70, 71, 75, 77, 86, 91, 96, 100: his family, 65-7, 68, 70
Ahriman, 113, 116
Ahuramazda, 108, 110, 111, 113-16
Alcohol among fireworshippers, 115-16: *see also* Arak
Alexander and the Kurds, 36
Ali and his line, 63-4
Ali Mohammed, the Bab, 78-81
Ali-Haq, 29, 30, 31
Anglo-Iranian Oil Company, 148
Arabs, 103, 107, 116: influenced by Persian culture, 94
Arak in Kerend, 25, 26: in Kerman, 112
Ararat, 11

Baghdad, Baha'u'llah in, 81
Baha'i faith, history, etc., 75-85
Baha'u'llah, 81-5
Baisger, 33, 34, 37-41
Baluchi refugees, 58, 61
Bandarabbas, 126, 132, 133-141
Bank of Agriculture, 121, 123
Bargaining, examples of, 14-15, 16, 17, 19
Beds not used, 22
Beggars, 17, 64-5
Bride price, Turkmen, 54
British sphere of interest, 145
Bunchag contract, 124-5
Burial, in Mashbad, 70
Buses, 14, 20, 127-8, 130
Butter churning, 33

Call to prayer, not used in Kerend, 23-4, 25
Carpet weaving, 91-3, 96-7, 98-9
Caspian Sea, 43, 45
Caviar, 46-7, 49, 50-1: the factory, 46-7
Chadur, prohibited by Reza Shah, 67: reappeared, 68
Child labour, 92-3, 96, 98-9
Children, believed to have been eaten, 136-7
Chi-yun, author's wife, *passim*
Clay for building, 18, 118, 126
Cleansing, ceremonial, 65, 68
Co-operatives, 121-2, 150-1
Costume, 16, 32, 33, 64: Turkmen, 59: in Bandarabbas, 126-7, 138
Cotton, 55, 57
Cyrus the Great, 20, 106-7

Dancing, 26, 27
Darius, 108: his inscription, 20
Disarming of tribes, 38-9

Index

Dishonesty, examples of, 12-13
Divorce, Baha'i and Mohammedan, 78
Dogs in Kerend, 23, 24
Dysentery, story of, cured by cannibalism, 136-7

Education, Baha'i views on, 78
Ekbatana, 20
Evil, view of, among Ali-Haq, 30, 31

Farming, 118-25
Fire worship, 29-31, 110-16
Fire-worshippers' abandoned temple, 129
Flood legend, 30
Flying, Kurdish legend of, 34

Genghis Khan and the Kurds, 36
Golam, a carpet-weaver, 96, 97-9
Graveyard in Kerend, 25-6
Gunbad Quabus, 52

Hamadan, 20
Hand crafts, 18, 33: *see also* Carpet weaving
Heroin, 73
Hitch-hiking, 12
Horses, Turkmen, 58-9
Hospitals, 99
Hotels, 15, 16, 19

Iran, name adopted, 37
Iraq and the Kurds, 36-7
Isfahan, the Bab at, 79: carpet weaving at, 91-3, 96-7, 98-9
Ishia, a carpet weaver, 93, 96

Jamshid, 109-17
Jewish beliefs, Persian in origin, 112

Kafekhanas, 93
Kampsax, 134, 135, 136
Kerend, 21-31, 39, 40
Kerman, 86: fire worship at, 110*ff*
Kurds, 11, 32-41: Shah's bodyguard composed of, 40
Kuwait, Persians work in, 127

Land, rent for, 119, 120, 125
Land, royal, 57, 58, 59-60
Land reform, 59-60, 120-5: no advantage, 39-41, 124: Shah's view of, 150-1
Life after death, belief among fire-worshippers, 112, 114, 115
Loans, interest on, 99, 122

Mashbad, 32, 62, 63, 64-5, 67-72, 75, 76
Meals, various, 16, 22, 24, 26, 66, 128
Military service, 41
Mohammed Jerangi, 86-90
Mohammed Reza Shah, 38, 142-3, 144, 146, 147, 149-52
Mosque in Kerend, 25
Mossadeq, 148-9
Mounds, burial?, 57
Moustaches in Kerend, 28

National character, 144
Nomads, 32-41

Oil, 148
Opium, addicts, 73: smoked by author, 72-4
Oven, an, 25
Oxen, hired, 121

Parsees, 116
Pepsi-Cola, 75
Persepolis, 101-5, 108
Persia and the Kurds, 37-8
Photography forbidden, 27, 138-9
Pilgrims in Mashbad, 70
Police, corrupt, 139-41: secret, 17
Postmaster makes a profit, 14-15, 17

Index

Prostitutes in Mashbad, 69

Quanats, 17, 63: stopped up, 122-3

Rashid, 11, 13-19
Religious toleration in ancient Persia, 105
Rent, 119, 120, 125
Reseta, 66-7
Reza Shah, 37, 55, 67, 68, 88, 146-7, 152
Robbers, 128, 129: Kurdish, 37-8: Turkmen, 52, 55, 56
Russian sphere of interest, 145, 147-8

Saadi, 42
Scorpion, belief about, 30
Secret police, 17
Seyyids, 64
Shaitan, 28, 30
Shah, belief in goodness of, 61
Shia sect, 63-4, 77, 86, 87
Shiraz, where Baha'ism started, 78, 79
Sigheh, 69
Slavery not known in ancient Persia, 104-5
Solomon, King, Kurdish legend of, 34
Story-teller, 94
Sturgeon fishing, 43-50
Sugar beet, 123

Tabriz, 17, 18
Taslimi, 52-6
Taxation of religious institutions, 71
Tea, 23, 53, 93
Teheran, 18, 37, 142
Tent, Kurdish, 33: Turkmen, 53
Timur and the Kurds, 36
Toilet paper not used, 16, 24
Tudeh, 148, 149
Turkey and the Kurds, 36
Turkish character, 12
Turkmenians, 52, 54-6, 58

Unbelievers, not allowed near mosque, 69

Veil (chadur), 67-8

Wages: earnings, 18, 58, 93, 98
Wahdet, Mr, 118-25
Water, lack of, 57, 122-3, 124, 128, 129, 137, 148: salty, 61
Wedding in Kerend, 26-8, 31
White underwear for fire-worshippers, 30
Women, Baha'i views on, 78: in Kerend, 21, 22, 24, 29, 31

Xenophon, on Kurds, 36: on Persian education, 105

Zarathustra, 111-16
Zarathustrians, 29: *see also* Fire worship